A FAITH OF ONE'S OWN

D0168238

A FAITH OF ONE'S OWN

Explorations by
Catholic Lesbians

EDITED BY BARBARA ZANOTTI

 THE CROSSING PRESS/Trumansburg, New York 14886

The Crossing Press Feminist Series.

Cover design and illustration: Diana Souza

Printed in the U.S.A.

Library of Congress Cataloging-in-Publication Data

A Faith of one's own.

   (The Crossing Press feminist series)
   1. Lesbians--Religious life. 2. Lesbianism--
Religious aspects--Catholic Church. 3. Catholic
Church--Doctrines. I. Zanotti, Barbara. II. Series.
BX2373.L46F35   1986   282'.08806643   86-16194

ISBN 0-89594-210-0
ISBN 0-89594-209-7 (pbk.)

Myrna, sweet love, this book is for you;
this blessing is for us.

with Beauty before us may we walk
with Beauty behind us may we walk
with Beauty above us may we walk
with Beauty all around us may we walk
with Beauty within us may we walk
in old age wandering on a Trail of Beauty
    lively may we walk
in old age wandering on a Trail of Beauty
    living again may we walk
it is finished in Beauty.

— Navaho Beauty Chant

Table of Contents

Acknowledgements

I am pleased to have this opportunity to express my deepest appreciation to the many women who have generously participated in the development of this anthology. My special thanks to Margaret Cruikshank who has been a wise friend and resourceful guide in the journey of this book. I thank Rosemary Ruether, Mary Hunt, Carter Heyward and Jeannine Gramick for their encouragement in the early stages of this project. For assistance in contacting Catholic lesbian women I thank Karen Doherty of the Conference for Catholic Lesbians, Joan Nestle and Deborah Edel of the Lesbian Herstory Archives, Luzma Umpierre, Maria Formoso and Nancy Manahan. For their life-giving friendship and spirited interest in my work I thank Christina Ouimet, Chris Loughlin and Anne Dellenbaugh. I thank my sister Jackie for showing me the meaning of courage and perseverance. Loving thanks to my children, Carolyn, Elizabeth, Stephen and David for holding faith with me. For nourishing this project and celebrating its progress, my thanks to the women in my friendship circle: Myrna, Randall, Jan, Betsy, Bev, Linda, Elizabeth, Karyn and Ginny. I especially honor Myrna Bouchey whose deep creativity, faithful assistance and Sapphic Friendship blessed this book from beginning to end. My appreciation to Kate Dunn of The Crossing Press for her confidence and enthusiasm. My abundant thanks to the contributors to this anthology for giving the gift of their experience to other lesbian searchers. Lastly, my deep thanks to the editors of, and contributors to, lesbian anthologies that have preceded this text. Their words and work gave inspiration to my own.

Introduction

The transformation of women's religious imagination has been a radical feature of second wave feminism.[1] With a critical feminist lens women have exposed and documented the inherent patriarchy and misogyny of religious institutions and have freed ourselves to explore our own spiritual consciousness. For lesbians raised in the Catholic household this self-affirming process involves a considerable sifting of experience since Catholicism is a multidimensional religious culture. When someone asks me, "Are you Catholic?" my reply is both no and yes. No, I am not a member of the institutional Catholic Church, but yes, Catholicism lives in my bones along with my working class origins and my mother's Irish heritage. Given the milieu in which I was raised and my own immersion in Catholic religious practice for thirty-seven years, in a very real sense I cannot not be Catholic; the imprint is simply and indelibly there. It is in this sense that the term Catholic is used in this text, to signify the religious/cultural background of lesbian contributors whether or not we avow Catholic religious commitments today.

This anthology has two related points of origin. Perhaps, most directly, it stems from my own need to trace the inner continuity of my life and stitch together the severed parts, but just as important, this text is rooted in conversations with other Catholic lesbians as we explored together the complexities of our dual identity. This book is an extension of those conversations, a further discussion of the varieties of Catholic lesbian faith.

In this context I am using the word faith to indicate an attitude of courage and confidence toward life itself, an affirmation which infuses existence with meaning and purpose. One instance of this faith is the compelling experience of Presence offered by Mary Mendola. Faith in these terms has nothing to do with assent to doctrine or adherence to commandments of any kind, nor belief in what cannot be understood, as religious convention teaches. Rather, lesbian faith is a woman-centered response to the world, springing from the passion of loving women and entrusting our energies to the values inspired by lesbian existence. What I am suggesting is that the freedom to enter the serpent (Gloria Anzaldúa), to break the chains of thought (Mev Miller) and to travel freely an open road (M. Cunningham) take their nourishment from the soil of lesbian faith.

Development of this collection involved considerable cor-
respondence between me and other contributors. I was frequently moved as lesbians recorded how strenuous the writing/
reflection/interpretation process was, but also how strengthening and self-validating the endeavor ultimately became.
Recognizing that invisibility and silence are dangerous and
disempowering, we shared a common desire to speak the truth
of our lives. Many of us understood our effort as a political act
of resistance, our contribution to lesbian memory/history which
we are determined to keep alive. The writing itself became an
expression of lesbian faith in ourselves, one another, and in the
value of our commitments.

The lesbian faith we embody stands in sharp contrast to the
patriarchal tradition into which we were born, a tradition whose
interpreters taught us to distrust our passions, to deny our
bodies and to surrender our energies to male interests in honor
of a male god. The impact of that conditioning is discussed by
Joy Christi Przestwor and Kathleen Meyer who record their
journeys through Catholic guilt and anxiety to their eventual
liberation as self-affirming lesbians. They disclose the damage
done to lesbian selves by the sanctified hetereosexual ethic while
illuminating the authentic grace of women-loving-women. They
write as survivors, as does Crystal Waverly whose essay exposes
the distortion and contradictions of Catholic education in the
fifties.

The devastating consequences of Catholic politics on women's
lives is a matter of public record.[2] Past and present efforts to
control women's bodies in the name of sacredness of life are
transparent machinations to secure male control of women and
to obscure the reality that women have always been the essential
tenders of life. In her brilliant work, *Beyond God the Father*,
Mary Daly exposed the real male trinity of rape, war and
genocide and since that historical event, masses of women have
undertaken the journey of exorcism and ecstasy to a space of our
own on the boundary of male institutions.[3] Julien Murphy continues this tradition of righteous female fury against the Church
by indicting the Church for systematic violence against women
and by insisting that lesbian wholeness requires coming out of
Catholicism.

As some of us made our exodus from the institution, another

women's movement began to evolve within Catholicism itself, expressed most dramatically by Women Church, a convergence of Catholic women's groups involved in a broad range of political struggles. As Mary Hunt details in her essay, these women claim to be Church, stating that the institutional hierarchy has betrayed the justice-seeking tradition which forms the center of Catholic life. Women Church members blend gospel and women's sources, use Christian and female symbols, and celebrate rituals which incorporate feminist and Catholic expressions. Jayne Young suggests the Women Church spirit in describing her initiation into Catholicism which had the distinct appearance of entering the Catholic lesbian sisterhood. As she asserts, "The Church is us." A similar perception is offered by Martha Courtot who renders a lesbian feminist interpretation of the sanctity of Maria Goretti, and who records her own journey back to Catholicism to claim for herself whatever value the tradition might hold. These writers define themselves as Catholic Christians on their own terms, selecting from their Catholic heritage those values which support their ideals of self and community. They declare that the Church is more than the institution and that the tradition is open to transformation in their hands. We see glimmers of that transformation in the theological reflections of Lorna Hochstein who concludes that women-loving women embody the divine and reveal something previously hidden about the nature of God.

At the core of the Women Church impulse is the issue of authority, a familiar shibboleth in Catholic circles. Contributors return to this theme repeatedly, marking our movement away from ecclesiastical pronouncements in order to respect the integrity of our conscience and to honor the wisdom of our body. Margaret Cruikshank reflects on this process as she claims for herself the right to define the meaning of her Catholic identity. Rejection of Church authority was a swift process for Hilda Hidalgo who recognized that there was no place for her in a sexist, homophobic church, and therefore she owed it no allegiance.

The strength of Church authority in exercising control over individual lives seems to come directly from the nature of religion itself. The word religion means to bind together, and the bonds of religious faith, for those who take them seriously, are as intimate as family ties. Belonging to a religious community generates a sense of social and cultural location and a solidarity born of a common religious vision. Altagracia Pérez Maceira depicts the communal power of Catholicism by exploring the significance of the Eucharistic ritual in strengthening the hopes and struggles of Puerto Rican Catholics. Similarly, Patt Saliba, writing from within the Maronite Rite, describes the social function of the Church in sustaining Lebanese customs and fostering Lebanese identity.

Historically the Catholic Church has succeeded in creating strong communities. There is an impressive record of religious orders of women and men, and within local parishes a variety of sodalities, societies and clubs. For the most part women have been the overwhelming majority in these associations, working to sustain the community and, in some instances, managing to develop their own lives.[4] In her essay, Joanne Still reminds us of the creativity, strength and intelligence of Catholic sisters who taught her to be free despite the restrictions of their own lives. Church leaders have recruited female energy, urging women to take our troubles to the altar and to trust in the wisdom of Catholic practice to bring safety and security to our lives. Like a family, our religious household encouraged our trust and welcomed our commitments. Because of the intimacy generated in religious community, a betrayal of trust by that community or its leaders is as shattering as betrayal by one's family. Jennifer Di Carlo unmasks just how deeply Catholicism has betrayed lesbians. The portrait she draws of invasive clerics seeking to define and expose her is chilling in its relevance. She insists that the Catholic Church is no safe place for women. While Pat O'Donnell also reports betrayal by manipulative clerics, she places the center of her religious community in a supportive group of friends, enabling her to affirm her gospel convictions and to condemn the hypocrisy of the hierarchy.

In distinguishing between institution and community, in contrasting the justice-seeking and women-hating aspects of Catholicism, and in identifying contradictions and characteristics of Catholic culture, contributors open up the complexity of Catholic experience. Patricia Novotny observes the multiplicity of Catholic lessons and interpreters. While she rejects the orthodoxy of the Church and stands outside the institution, she affirms certain habits of heart and mind bequeathed by her Catholic training. In somewhat the same way, Mab Maher explores three attitudes of her soul which are transformed remnants of her Catholic past. In contrast to these writers, Linda Marie humorously records that her only leftover from Catholicism is a compulsion to reveal her secret acts.

While the diversity of Catholic lesbian experience is reflected in these essays, it is far from exhausted. These are the journeys of some Catholic lesbians, almost all from the United States. Other voices from within and beyond this country could extend the range of experience significantly. We are helped to think broadly by Fulana de Tal who reminds us of the enforced hidden life of lesbians in Argentina, and by Mary Moran who presents fictionalized letters which expose the painful quandary of an ex-Catholic Argentine lesbian living in the U.S. illegally. Moran places lesbian love within the context of sisterhood, showing that lesbian survival depends on the strength of the women's movement.

The necessity of a strong women's movement to support lesbian existence is commonly acknowledged. Because we are invisible or caricatured in patriarchy, lesbians depend on ourselves and other women to nourish our reality. Abundant lesbian energy has gone into the creation of women's culture precisely because we need gynocentric culture to reflect and celebrate our woman-centered world. Lesbians have also learned that, for the most part, we can only depend on ourselves to assert our right to exist.[5] Though we may participate in other political struggles our oppression is often omitted in the catalog of changes worth fighting for. Carol Seajay's eloquent coming out narrative illustrates how crucial lesbian community is, particularly for younger lesbians. Her poignant story reminds us that our lives are a legacy to coming generations of lesbians.

Karen Doherty's creative storytelling of the founding of the Conference for Catholic Lesbians also resounds with an emphasis on community and continuity. She explores how that gathering and subsequent organization gives validation to the particularities of Catholic lesbian identity and is a new moment in lesbian and Catholic history. Though very different in their response to Catholicism, both authors concur in the need for lesbians to create an environment in which we can be all of who we are.

As lesbians raised in the Catholic household we were taught that the Church would teach us who we were to be, but in our own odysseys we discovered something radically different: that

in our love for women we came home to ourselves. Maggie Redding catches the dynamism of the journey in tracing her own
voyage from Catholic motherhood to lesbian existence. Her narrative is double-edged, disclosing the multiple oppressions of
women in the nuclear family and the particular jeopardy of lesbian mothers. As she and her lover take up a simple rural life,
the reader is once again reminded of the condition of lesbians as
outsiders.

As many of us have come to experience, there are both
negative and positive features in this situation. Among the
negative consequences recorded here are public hatred, job loss,
silencing, invisibility, psychological labelling and the loss of
family and friends. Developing the survival skills needed to
stand outside does, however, offer surprising positive results:
from the outside looking in we are able to see the oppressive
structure of patriarchy with considerable clarity and, having no
investment in patriarchal society, we are free to create ourselves.
Valerie Miner explores these themes in her poignant story of
Sophia, whose life is discounted, unseen and unheard. As
Sophia turns away from family and town and moves toward her
own face mirrored in the shining sea, we glimpse the journey
many lesbians have made. Strangers in the land of the fathers,
we birth a world of our own.

Here, then, are the voices in this collection. I invite you to
hear our words and celebrate our faith.

Barbara Zanotti
Summer Solstice 1986

1. Foresisters in the nineteenth century also concerned with issues of women and
religion include Matilda Joslyn Gage, *Women, Church and State* (c. 1893;
reprint edition Watertown, MA: Persephone Press, 1980) and Elizabeth Cady
Stanton, *The Woman's Bible, Part I.* (New York: European Publishing Company, 1898. Reprint edition by Coalition Task Force on Women and Religion.
Seattle, WA, 1974).

2. The statistics supplied in *Sisterhood is Global* edited by Robin Morgan (New
York: Anchor Books, 1984) provide a comprehensive and devastating account of
the impact of Church laws on women's lives.

3. My deep appreciation to Mary Daly whose Haggard Musings inspire my
journey.

4. For an excellent historical account of women's work in the churches see *Women and Religion in America,* edited by Rosemary Radford Ruether and Rosemary Skinner Keller, volumes I and II (San Francisco: Harper and Row, 1981 & 1984).

5. See the critical essays of Julia Penelope regarding lesbian survival ("The Mystery of Lesbians") in volumes 1-3 of *Lesbian Ethics.*

Blessed Are Lesbians Who Search the Spirit They Will Find Her in Themselves

Having unlearned the tendency to place our faith outside ourselves and having rejected the authoritarianism of Catholicism, Catholic lesbians are re-naming religious symbols, re-interpreting religious values, and re-defining religious experience. As we explore the fullness of lesbian identity we grow into a faith of our own in which spirituality and sexuality become one. Our religious search leads us home to ourselves enlarging our capacity to embody and communicate the presence of Spirit.

The Conference for Catholic Lesbians

Karen Doherty

"Who made you?"
"God made me."
"Did God make all things?"
"Yes, God made all things."
"What is sin, Miss Doherty?"
"There are two kinds of sin, Sister. Moral and venereal."
"*Mortal and venial*, Miss Doherty. Mortal and venial."

One of my friends in sixth grade was Eileen Bernstein. We were Girl Scouts together and on Tuesday after school we walked uptown for the meeting of Troop #12. On Wednesday our paths separated: Eileen went to Hebrew School and I went to Catholic confirmation class. Sometimes we talked about what it was like to be Catholic or Jewish. One of the things that really puzzled me was why Jewish people couldn't eat pork.

"Eileen, what's it like to know you have to go your whole life without ever having bacon and eggs for breakfast?" I couldn't imagine it.

She said: "About the same as having to go your whole life eating fish sticks every Friday night."

Stories and myths are a necessary part of our religious tradition. Because they entertain and instruct, inspire and comfort, they are important threads in our cultural and spiritual fabric. Traditions are the accumulation of many stories, many images. They carry what uniquely belongs to a people from one generation to another.

The story I would like to tell, a favorite that I've repeated many times to friends around the country, is about the Conference for Catholic Lesbians. Remembering my storytelling and the nights it took place, I see faces around a kitchen table and feel the common pulse of lesbian women creating our history. I hear the first Kirkridge gathering relived as each woman recalls her experience and those who were not there add a special memory from their own lives. Throughout these marvelous nights the story expanded until we were all part of it.

My road to Kirkridge began in high school when I was playing CYO (Catholic Youth Organization) basketball. The basketball team, in turn, had its roots in the Sodality Club. One day, during a break in our Sodality meeting, some of us snuck off to the gym to shoot a few baskets. Suddenly, a figure loomed in the doorway — Sister Mary Andrew. "Do you girls want to play basketball or go to Sodality?"

"Play basketball," we yelled with one voice and heart.

Sister Mary Andrew's response: she coached the team to the championship three years running. I remember that when our team prayed together in a huddle just before the opening of the championship game I felt the connection of fierce love — so different a connection than we shared during our days as Sodalites in that grey church basement.

Sometimes when I go home for Christmas I return to the gym. Our trophy — Grand Champions, 1970 — dominates the trophy display over the gym door. The late afternoon sun shines through the windows, just as I remember. If I listen hard enough, I can hear the yells and cries of encouragement, hear those white Keds squeaking, and the rosary beads clicking as the coach dribbles the ball down the court and gets past me to make a shot.

I don't know what took hold of me to bring me to the conference at Kirkridge. Perhaps it was the need to express myself, or to answer a challenge, or simply a desire to huddle with other women again, praying for victory.

At the closing liturgy of the conference I sat staring down at the rug, not wanting to look up, afraid women would see how much I cared. It reminded me with a start of how I used to act as a kid in church — looking at my money, looking at someone's hands praying — never looking up at God. I wanted God to know how angry I was about being in church. I hated to wear a dress and hat. I hated having my prayers ruined by the steady pace of Catholic ritual. One time, I went so far as to stay kneeling, with my fingers in my ears, but I felt so odd and alone I never did it again. To make doubly sure God knew, I pretended I didn't care. In the end I just stopped praying.

The reason I continue to identify myself as Catholic is something of a mystery to me. There is every reason to view today's Church with fury and frustration. The oppressive second class status of women in Catholicism is a continuing source of deep alienation. Why do I continue to care? I suspect the answer is really quite simple: if I were to renounce it all I would have to renounce my memories as well, but because they are so integral to my life, it would be impossible to let them go.

Like vigil lights, for instance. A few years ago when I was visiting my family I walked over to the parish church where I had received the sacraments of Baptism, Eucharist and Confirmation. The place still smelled like candlewax. The weekly bulletin still advertised funeral homes, car dealerships, and bakeries. My eyes were drawn to the vigil lights, flickering in front of the altar. I was reminded of how my sister and I would light candles for our relatives who had passed away. I understood that lighting candles generally meant a reduced sentence in Purgatory, but even as a child I was well acquainted with my family's colorful history and not fooled that one small candle could have any impact. Instead we would light candles in remembrance, a way to say hello to Aunt Florence, Gramsey, Mother's Mother and everyone else.

Once again I went up to the stand, put quarters in the slot, lit my candles and began to pray: "It's been a long time since I've been to church. Since then I graduated from college, moved to Alaska, got divorced and came home. I love you and think of you often." Stunned, I started to cry. The communion of saints — the unity of the dead and the living — still has power for me. I slipped through the side door of the church and looked back at the candles. They were flickering with amazing brilliance.

In May of 1981, my lover, Christine, and I attended a retreat for lesbians sponsored by New Ways Ministry. We fought every mile of the way. She wanted to go; I didn't. Thank heaven she insisted. The idea of a national meeting of Catholic lesbians was first discussed during that retreat. It was a thought I carried home with me. By February 1982, it had gathered enough momentum so that a group met to draw up plans for a conference to be held later that year. The conference, from which the organizational name is taken, convened at Kirkridge in

Bangor, Pennsylvania in November 1982. More than one hundred women attended that historic gathering, coming from many states and provinces (one woman even came from Argentina).

Nothing could have prepared me for the feeling of seeing one hundred women just like me. When women bestowed on one another their kiss of peace at the closing liturgy which women led, some lesbians wept openly, crying for a time once dimly hoped for, but now realized.

The impetus for the conference came from the fact that none of the groups we might have belonged to — women's, Catholic, or lesbian — spoke sensitively to the needs of Catholic Lesbians. None encouraged activities relating to our identity — either social or spiritual. In many cases, our presence wasn't acknowledged at all. There was a need for Catholic Lesbians to come together publicly as Catholic Lesbians.

The deeply felt need that emerged from Kirkridge and which was expressed in an outpouring of letters that followed the event was for a network through which Catholic Lesbians could be in touch with one another. Three months after the initial conference, the organizers met once again — to form the Conference for Catholic Lesbians.

Wasn't there ever a gathering of Catholic Lesbians before? Wasn't Lesbianism ever public in the Church prior to 1982? It seems hard to believe we have had to wait 2,000 years for it to happen. We will never know how much of our history has been lost simply because we have not been its writers or guardians, or because we have never been in the position to pass down our stories, retelling them at our anniversaries and celebrations. To tell the story of CCL is to create something more precious than a bare list of dates and names. It is to spin a history, the way writers of the Bible created their myths, and poets and troubadours sang of great adventure.

The story of CCL is important, not only in Church history, but in Lesbian history as well. We are now visible, real enough to be remembered, the way Sappho is held in memory as teacher and lover, the way the Amazons are remembered as a proud and independent race of warriors. The first meeting at Kirkridge, the founding of CCL, has become a sacred story. It will pass beyond its time to live in the memory of all who speak of it and who believe in it. It is a story heard not only from women who were there, but from friends of those who were, and friends of friends — passed along from one woman to another, the connection from the creation to the word unbroken, as each woman adds her own dreams, images, and ideals.

Mirroring God

Lorna Hochstein

Ultimate Reality must always be encountered in
earthly events if it is to matter at all.
—D. Austin[1]

God did not create lesbians as a diversion, on a whim or by
accident. There is something deliberate and meaningful about
lesbian love, something ultimately and ontologically purposeful.
Lesbians bring the Catholic Church, the Christian tradition and
anyone willing to listen a message about the nature of God. We
are, perhaps, a minority report, but the lives of lesbian women
are God's Word through time, across cultures.

Christianity is an incarnational religion. Christians believe
that God became a human person, that through the human
presence of Jesus, God was manifested to the world. Through
Jesus, divinity entered into a concrete relationship with other
created selves. It is in and through that relation that God's
nature is revealed to the world. The person Jesus from Nazareth
died, but Christian belief informs us that God continues to be
revealed to the world in an on-going way through the lives and
relationships of human persons. Jesus, an embodied human
man, was God's Word to the world. So each of us, too, com-
municates something of God to others in and through our
body/selves. As we are able to encounter God in Jesus, so we are
each able to encounter God and experience the divine most profoundly through our loving relationships with other such
body/selves.

All people communicate bodily. I do not live with and love a
spirit; I live with and love an embodied flesh and blood woman.
As I communicate something of God to my lover thru my work,
play and lovemaking, so she reveals something of God's nature
to me. This communication, this revelation, is both emotional

and physical. God uses body/selves to share God's own self with the world. God *needs* body/selves to share Herself with the world. Finally, God needs lesbian body/selves to share Her own self with the Church and with the world.

Self-disclosure is essential to the life, depth and growth of any human or divine being. Making oneself known to that same self and to other selves is essential to the life, depth and growth of every human-human and human-divine relationship. It is this sharing of personal knowledge and insight with one's own self, with God and with other persons which allows us to become spiritual women.

First we must share the knowledge of our lesbianism with our own selves. Seven years ago, on a warm June evening, I walked on the banks of the Charles River with a friend and we talked. I turned to her, finally, and demanded that she kiss me. She did, and I knew then that I was one of those women we had been discussing so intently. That realization remained clear for the next twenty-four hours, and I was happy. Later, fears and doubts assailed that incredible clarity and I plunged into eighteen months of radical estrangement and paralyzing uncertainty, alienation and pain. I struggled with this piece of self-knowledge and with a marriage I knew I must end. I was twenty-five years old, actively Catholic, married for four years and beginning graduate work in psychology. I had made a tentative peace with my family and I felt content. I was not expecting the confrontation with truth that began that night. My awareness of my very being changed.

Prior to that time, I was not a particularly spiritual person. Although I was interested in the Catholic Church, in God and in the Bible, and although I often attended Mass and received the sacraments, my interest lacked passion and genuine connection to that source of creation and sustainer of life I call God. I lacked a primary connection to myself, and thus, I lacked a primary connection to God.

I had successfully kept my lesbianism a secret from my own self; I had not allowed my soul to speak to my conscious mind. Since I was unable to share this deepest being with my conscious self, I could not share it with others. My unknowing self-estrangement had limited the openness, trust, love and vitality I felt within myself and so it limited the degree of openness, trust, love and vitality I could bring to any relationship with another person or with God. I was not, in fact, a spiritual person. The self-deception by which I thought myself a woman who was most deeply fulfilled by loving men limited the potential for connectedness within myself and between myself and others. I could only become a spiritual person when I acknowledged that God had created me lesbian and that because of my primary emotional, spiritual and physical love for women, I live and love and experience God in a special, particular way. I experience God most profoundly in my love for other women.

Lesbian women become more deeply spiritual women when we acknowledge that God created us lesbian and that as lesbians, we mirror God to each other, to the Church, and to the world uniquely. Our self-disclosure is God's self-disclosure; our silence is God's silence.

The patriarchal tradition of the Catholic Church has erased, denied and trivialized all women's experiences, virtually destroying our attempts at self-knowledge and self-expression. It has thereby kept generations of women in an unspiritual state. By refusing all Christian women (especially women-loving women) the means of self-knowledge, patriarchal Christianity has denied itself and the world knowledge of God. But acknowledgement of a woman's lesbianism to her own self is only the first step toward a spiritual life. To be spiritual women, to mediate the presence of God to others, we must acknowledge to ourselves *and to others* that we are lesbian. Such self-disclosure is essential for the life and growth of each lesbian woman and for her relationships with others. Such self-disclosure is essential for the continuing growth of God's presence in women's lives and in the life of the world.

Everyone cares when a woman professes love for another woman. Patriarchy has decreed that women shall love men, and punishment for disobedience has been severe. And so, for good and necessary reasons, lesbians often choose not to expose our woman-love. The silence may be necessary, but the choice for silence limits the possibility for God's creative presence in the world.

A disclosure of one's love of women or, more typically, of one's love for a particular woman, does not always yield "happy" results. I had labelled myself lesbian for several years before sharing that orientation with my parents. I was involved in a committed relationship; my lover and I owned a home and two

cats and had a circle of gay, lesbian and straight friends.
Everyone close to me knew of my love relationship — everyone
except my parents. I hated the evasions and the withholding of
information which seemed to constitute lies. I had never shared
with my parents the cause of my depression and distance as I
struggled through accepting my lesbian self and I had never
stated that my lesbianism was a major reason for my divorce. I
had never explained my obvious closeness to my women friends,
my commitment to feminism, or my rage at patriarchal society.
So much of what I did and said made no sense without these ex-
planations. Long before my mother directly asked about my sexual orientation, I knew that, when she did, I would cease the
evasions and tell the truth. And I did. It would have been easier
not to, easier for them and for me. But the pretense was stifling
and I knew that the longer I kept silent the more distant I would
feel from them, the more contempt I would have for their blind-
ness, and the more anger I would feel at my own cowardice.
When my mother asked if I were a lesbian, I said I was. Two
years later neither of my parents mention my lover's name. I go
to their home alone. My mother (and, presumably, my father)
feels that my lover has ruined my life. This self-disclosure has
not had happy results. There is much about my life that I have
not shared; there is much they do not wish to know. At least the
possibility for such honest sharing is present now. I am only
occasionally evasive. In many ways my parents still do not know
who I am or what I am about. They do not know because they
have chosen not to ask or to hear, not because I have refused to
tell them. They have the information they need to know and
understand the choices I have made whenever they choose to use
it. Painful though this response has been, I am glad that my
mother asked and that I told. When I acknowledged my love of
a woman I helped clear space for the possibility of truth, openness, trust and love, for the possibility of God's presence
between us in a new way. God, too, loves women.

Our Catholic Christian belief has informed and influenced the
way each of us perceives and experiences our life and our love of
women. We each know how Catholic dogma has contributed to
our past or present image of ourselves as wrong, sick, sinful, im-
mature, perverse people, as women less valuable to the Church
and the world than are women who primarily love men.
Sometimes we have gotten so stuck in this self-denigrating mire

that we have forgotten another fact. That is, that while we are each influenced by Catholic doctrine concerning sexuality, our experience of loving women can inform Catholic Christian belief. Our willingness to believe others' assessment of lesbians has led us to deny a part of ourselves and a part of God. It has allowed others and ourselves to continue to portray God in exclusively heterosexual images. It allows us to deny the basic truth that all of us, female or male, lesbian, gay or heterosexual, image God. If we allow for the possibility of love between women, we allow for a new image of God. If we deny that love, we create a limited, idolatrous God whose being is mediated only by heterosexual women and men.

What does lesbian love reveal about God? A woman's love for another woman, a woman's serious commitment to relationship with another woman presents a continuing sign that with God all things are possible. Emotional and sexual love between women exists despite all lack of validation, recognition, affirmation and active fostering. It continues to exist despite strenuous attempts to destroy it or degrade it. The on-going existence of woman-love is a dramatic sign that God's presence is possible anywhere, any time, and that hopelessness is not ever justified. It is a sign that any desire to cease struggling for truthfulness in our relationships with others must not be indulged. God's creative love is sturdier, stronger, more creative, flexible and enduring than any warrior, judge, almighty, powerful, father God could ever be.

Enduring though this presence is, love between two women also conveys the vulnerability of God's presence. Such presence is easily affected by a touch of cowardice; silent lies can stifle its growth. Lesbian relationships remind the world of the price of integrity. Lesbian relationships can embody intense strength, and resistance to all attempts at eradication, as well as a serious vulnerability to secrecy and ungenuineness.

Love between women reminds us that God calls us to love deeply the most unlikely people. My struggle to accept my physical and emotional love of a woman taught me that I place limitations on whom I would love. I had placed limitations on where I would allow God to be present. I have learned that an act of lovemaking can be as sacramental as the breaking of bread. God does show Herself in unexpected places!

Love between women reminds the world that God's Word exists independently of current trends or prejudices, independent of any audience for that Word. While often ignored and rendered invisible, lesbians themselves do not go away. Finally, a glimpse of two women in love is a gratuitous gift from God, a miracle of courage, daring and integrity. Such a sight is a delight offered by God to those able to see.

Lesbian spirituality resembles Christian spirituality when it is visionary, sacramental, relational and transformational.[2] One woman's love for another is possible only if she is willing and able to perceive reality/God in a new way at odds with the predominant culture around her. It is possible only if she is willing and able to create a life which concretizes that new vision of a woman-centered relationship. As creations of God, lesbians are imbued with the spirit of God and are mediators of the divine. Our love for each other relates us to God and brings us to God; it can bring God to others, whether they are gay, or nongay. Love between women heals, renews, brings joy, sustains hope and allows us to touch God through our touch of one another. Being lesbian invites a woman to live out the knowledge that there is more to life than meets the eye. In so doing, we enflesh the divine. Women who love women are indeed fortunate to have been set apart for such delight.

1. Austin, D. "On becoming a theologian: In praise of the ordinary life." *Harvard Divinity Bulletin,* Oct.-Nov. 1982, *13* (1), 14-16.

2. McBrien, R. *Catholicism* vol. 2. New York: Winston Press, 1980, pp. 1057-1058.

Passing Through
the Eye of a Needle

Mary Mendola

December 1984: I receive a letter from BZ — she wants to compile an anthology of writings by Catholic lesbians. So why is she writing to me? I'm not Catholic anymore.

January 1985: I'm in Portland, Maine — by accident (any January in Portland is an accident). BZ does a five-hour drive through sub-zero weather to talk to me about my Catholic heritage and the influence it has on my current life. It doesn't have any, so instead we talk through the night about the structure of her book, feminism, Harvard, raising kids, and raising parents.

September 1985: I get another letter from BZ. October 31 is the deadline for my Catholic heritage and the influence it has on my life today. I shove the letter into my attache case, and I'm out the door racing to catch up with "my life today."

Late for a videotape editing session. Can't get a taxi. Take a city bus to the studio for another day of watching the world on "fast forward." Catholicism has nothing to do with my life today...unless, perhaps, I can "freeze-frame" today and do a "reverse scan" on old tapes.

I'm on the bus — I'll do it now. Bouncing over city potholes: don't be afraid, play the old tapes. Okay, roll Catholicism. Chubby little girl in a white First Communion dress; fish on Friday; confession on Saturday; Mass on Sunday, and a meatball at my Aunt Rosalie's house on the way home from *Tantum Ergo*. Stop tape. Catholicism has no influence on my life today, and there's no room in my life for Catholicism.

The bus is moving too slowly downtown. It's not one of the new "kneeling" buses, and two elderly people are struggling to help each other up that first high step. Stop for a light: there's a man sitting on the corner begging for change. I wonder where he left his legs. The light changes, and the bus is moving again — past the city's growing population of homeless bag people, past the drugged and the drunk whom I sometimes envy for having relinquished their right to see. See what? See what I see when I hear myself saying, "Goddamn, there's a Cosmic Christ on every street corner in Manhattan."

Sunday morning: Cutting the grass in Brooklyn. My mother is calling to me from the kitchen window: "Come in, it's almost time for The Peace." I sit with her at the kitchen table, and together we watch the rest of the electronic Mass being televised for people who are too old or too sick or too tired to walk to their parish churches. People who, unlike me, still believe in Catholicism.

"I like when you're here on Sunday for the Kiss of Peace," she says. "It's not nice when I'm here alone and there's nobody to kiss."

And then the television priest says, "Turn to each other now, and offer the Kiss of Peace." And my mother and I kiss, and then we sit watching communicants walk to the cardboard altar as the studio priest says again and again, "Body of Christ."

When I sit there holding my mother's hand, I touch Presence. Because we, together, are my Cosmic Christ, my Cosmic Whole, my Cosmic Yahweh. And we are one with the elderly couple struggling to climb onto the bus. We are one with the man who left his legs somewhere. We are one with the homeless. We are one with the drugged and the drunk. We are one with the other *schmucks* like me — the demographically upper-middle- or upper-income, highly mobile, upscale types who are out there on the street, as scared as everybody else, trying to survive in our particular jungle of choices. And in touching my mother, I touch all of them, I touch myself — because we are, all together, one with my Cosmic Whole.

And then Mass is over, it's time for a commercial, she makes me coffee, and the script is always the same. "You used to be a nun," she says, "now you're a heathen." I don't tell her that, based on her definition of heathen, I became one while I was a nun. I do deny being a heathen, and I do try to explain to her that I am more religious now than I've probably ever been before in my life.

"But you don't go to church," she says. "How can you say you're religious? What's your religion? Tell me."

I explain that I don't have a religion. "See, you're a heathen," she concludes. "Heathens don't have a religion. And you don't go to see your father in the cemetery, either."

"Mom, I don't have to go to the cemetery to see Dad. He's not there."

"Yeah, and you don't have to go to church to see God. I know, I know. Don't start that stuff with me — you confuse me. If you respected your father, you'd go to the cemetery."

The "stuff" she doesn't want me to start is all the "stuff" I haven't yet been able to explain to her, because it in no way relates to the Catholic heritage in which she raised me. Like sometimes, late in the afternoon, when the cellar in Brooklyn is wrapped in shadows with the last rays of a Saturday sun, my father and I are one there. I lay my hands on his workbench, and I can feel his presence. And his presence and mine are one with the Cosmic Presence. He and I, together, are the same breath being breathed throughout the streets of Brooklyn and Manhattan and Pakistan and China and Nicaragua and South Africa. We breathe the same universal breath — we who are alive in the flesh and we who are alive in one universal soul. That's my Cosmic Whole.

No, I can't tell my mother that my father, who has been dead for four years, is really in the basement. I have enough problems dealing with her Italian-Catholic superstitions. Nor can I tell her that when I'm working in the yard, playing with the same dirt, that Brooklyn earth, that my father played with for almost 50 years, he and I are one. But then I also can't tell her how, when I walk through the streets of Manhattan, I am sometimes one with the forgotten who left home without their American Express cards.

I can't share with my mother, or too many other people, my experience of Presence. My earliest recollections of these experiences: they hit me somewhere between the ages of 11 and 12, and everywhere between the sidewalks of Brooklyn and the mountains of upstate New York. I don't think I was consciously aware of them, anymore than children are aware they need glasses until someone tells them they do. By the time I became consciously aware of the experiences, I was already a problem student and a problem teenager. I wasn't about to tell anyone anything that was going to make me a problem something-else. Later, my three years in religious life were tumultuous enough without adding this other dimension.

And so I kept my secret until my late 20s. Then, whenever I tried to describe it to my closest friends, they'd ask if I was on drugs. The secret went into a time capsule to be opened in another decade.

I came out of the spiritual closet when I no longer needed to remain hidden. In my own process of becoming, I found that I no longer feared nonacceptance. I realized finally that if I couldn't relate to religious rituals, prayer groups, or feminist liturgies, it wasn't because there was something wrong with me or because I didn't experience the richness of a spiritual life. It was — and is — because my spiritual experiences and needs are different. I no longer apologize for not needing or experiencing what others may need or experience. And I don't try to hide it anymore.

The wonderful part about my spiritual coming out is that the more open I have become with people, the more open people have become in sharing their own, similar spiritual experiences with me. These people have shaped for me what I call my spiritual community. My spiritual community doesn't have a name, nor do its members share a particular religious background or orientation. We don't meet regularly, and most of them have never met each other. The one thing I share with each of them is a similar spiritual life. We believe in nothing, so we are free to believe in everything. We share an experience of Cosmic Presence.

For each of them, it's a different experience. I can only talk about mine. All of a sudden, in a second, I experience a presence of power, and lost in that presence, I don't know whether that second lasted a second — or an hour. I become wrapped in silence and stillness.

I've spoken with people who have also experienced this presence of power. Some are, as I was, afraid of it. It becomes threatening because they feel absorbed and consumed by another reality. I've often heard it expressed this way, "I'm afraid I won't come back." I've moved beyond being afraid of it. Now I seek it out and embrace it as a sustaining force in my life. I wouldn't want to live in the world I know without it. It is

an experience of a loving power, the intensity of which makes
the conference rooms of corporate power seem feeble — silly.

It also makes me seem feeble and silly in my own eyes, because
when I experience Cosmic Presence, I am nothing. There is no
individuality, no personality, no ambition — there's no *anything*
but awareness of Presence. That total loss of self is no longer
frightening to me, because it is that loss of self that enables me
to be present to — and to become part of — another reality, a
greater whole.

Is my Cosmic Christ an *outgrowth* of my Catholic Heritage? I
don't know. But, thank God (or whomever), my Cosmic Christ
survived Catholicism. He/she/it permeates every aspect of my
life. My Cosmic Christ is stillness, and it is peace. It is trust in a
higher order beyond the disorder I see. It is a refuge called
silence. It is my being present to Presence.

Is that a lower-case *p* or upper-case *P* for Presence? I type it in
upper case, but it doesn't really matter. Gender masculine,
feminine? I leave that to the theologians. Attributing a gender to
the power of the spirit I experience seems ludicrous. I don't
know, and truthfully, I don't have time to care. Give it a name,
or don't give it a name. All I know is that it *is.*

Is this all *part* of my Catholic heritage? I don't know. Is it the
influence of Chardin and Merton? (Were they Catholic, or is
that still being debated by the Church?) Is it mysticism? Self-
hypnosis? Psychosis? Again, I don't know, but what's more important is that I don't *have* to know anymore. What does all of
this make me? Perhaps it qualifies me as "lunatic fringe." And
that's okay. To me, it makes me who I am: at 41, a hard-
working, hard-playing, Scotch-drinking, lusty contemplative.

I no longer consider myself a member of the Catholic Church.
But I wouldn't miss one televised interview with His Eminence
of the New York Archdiocese, Cardinal John Statesman O'Con-
nor. My rage chains me to the One, Holy, Catholic, and
Apostolic Church. And when I walk past St. Patrick's Cathedral
during the Gay Pride Parade, what I'm not proud of are the
guard dogs and the mounted police positioned in front. The ra-
tionale in this annual display of unified Church and State power:
the police and dogs are there so that "they" don't sully the
cathedral by their presence on the steps. "They" must be kept
away, must not involve the Church in their arrogant display of

"pride" in what the Church has decided, in God's name, is "sin." I ache at that level of ecclesiastical ignorance and violence. Do I ache because of my Catholic heritage? Because something that was so much a part of my life for so long — and so important, at least at the time — is capable of such ugliness? Or do I ache because the "they" being prevented from sullying the cathedral is *me*? Because I once believed it when I was told I was a "daughter" of the Church, and I am again faced with proof that the institutional Church is nobody's mother? Because the institutional Church is no different than the sexist corporations I deal with every day. The men enthroned in both these institutions only accept women who agree to be shaped in the image and likeness of what the power brokers dictate women should be. They only accept people, in general, who agree to play the game in *their* ballpark — and by *their* rules.

To say I am no longer a practicing Catholic is to say I no longer practice digestion. Catholicism is as much a part of my system as my digestive tract — the former produces emotional nausea and intellectual vomiting when swallowed with rage. The latter keeps me running as long as I supply it with all that good stuff our mothers made us eat.

What does my Catholic heritage have to do with my life today? Nothing. And everything. Nothing in terms of my spiritual life. Everything in terms of the cultural and religious life I share with people I love who still believe in Catholicism.

There's a letter on file with my attorney that says if I die before my mother, her only daughter will be buried in her Catholic heritage. It also says that if I die *after* my mother, I will be buried, period. Because whether I am buried Catholic or buried merely dead, I become one with my Cosmic Presence, absorbed with my Cosmic Christ, and part of the breath we all breathe, the one soul we all share. And that's my Cosmic Whole, my Yahweh.

And it sure as hell better be there, because my Catholic heritage afterlife is not *my* idea of heaven.

Este Es Mi Cuerpo[1]

Altagracia Pérez Maceira

The relationship was over. At age sixteen that's not an odd experience, but something felt wrong. At that moment I felt gripped by an overwhelming sadness. Was I different from other girls? Would I ever be able to have the kind of relationship I desired? I went to my bed, the bottom half of a bunkbed I shared with my younger sister, and I cried. I rocked back and forth hugging my pillow. God the Father, the only god I knew at the time, came and held me. He rocked me back and forth and told me He loved me. I fell asleep.

The relationship was over. I couldn't deny the truth anymore. I knew that he was not what I wanted. I wanted her. She wanted me. By this point I knew God did not think it was dirty or wrong. All the years I had tortured myself with thoughts of demons of lesbianism lurking in my room were over. I knew that much. But could I come out? Could I leave the security of a perfectly "normal" acceptable life? I ran to the park. I knew I could find God the Mother there. Faithful as fresh rain she came. She told me that I need not fear; I was a woman with strength and power, who would live with truth and integrity. I walked home with new resolve.

The relationship is growing. I hold her in my arms and kiss her soft skin everywhere. We make love, opening ourselves to each other in a way I never thought possible. We embrace and our communion delights us. As I close my eyes I see God, a Spirit of power and light. I feel strengthened and refreshed in the love I have found. My God is now reflected in that love and in our struggles.

From time to time I recall my own spiritual journey. As I have a developed a fuller understanding of myself, my conceptions of God, Christianity and religion have changed. To the degree that I have put together the various parts of my being — Puerto

Rican, Woman, Black, Poor, Lesbian, Christian, etc. — the clearer my vision of God has become. Exploring this process is critical to my understanding of spirituality.

Catholicism is one of the elements that has contributed to my identity. Within the Puerto Rican community (especially in the lower economic strata which comprises the majority of Puerto Ricans), Catholicism is usually described as a syncretistic popular religiosity. For most of us, it is a spirituality which interweaves Catholic, African and indigenous elements. This combination of religious traditions and practices has led to a religious worldview which is adaptable to different needs. For the majority of Puerto Rican Catholics there seems to be no need to differentiate and choose from these traditions.

In any given Puerto Rican home one will find an altar graced by the usual crucifix, rosary beads, and a few identifiable saints. In addition, however, are El Indio (the Indian), who is the guard of the home, and other statues which are not part of the communion of Catholic saints. There are glasses of water, bowls of pennies, pieces of bread and fruit, and a conglomeration of other gifts offered to God and the saints. Members of the family pray and offer gifts that their friends be healed, that a job interview go well, or that their number might hit. It is not uncommon to go to confession on Friday, visit the Espiritista (the Spiritualist) on Saturday, and attend Mass on Sunday. There is no contradiction implicit in these activities; God is a big God and human beings need all the help they can get in communicating with the powers that be. Furthermore, priests are not seen as having a corner on the market when it comes to communicating with God — plenty of people, female and male, receive this gift. Having been raised with this religious world view I believe that God and religion are ecstatic not static; rigorous, not rigid. This dynamism allows space to redefine old symbols so that they become meaningful given a community's experience. This fluidity is what defines our Catholicism, and it so happens that our ability to be fluid is critical to our survival in this country.

The Puerto Rican people in the United States, as with most Hispanics in this country, are a pilgrim people who move in hopes of finding a better life for themselves and their families. This is our history and our heritage. Our parents were forced to leave their island because of economic destabilization caused by colonialism. We carry the stigma of being alien and being unable to claim a distinctive country and culture. Penetration by North America is pervasive, but an undying Spirit empowers us to claim our identity as Puerto Ricans. We endure because we are a communal people. This means that family — and this is not limited to the nuclear family — is crucial to our existence. Our communities help us to maintain our identity, to tell our stories, and to live our lives, however marginal.[2]

Sharing a meal within Puerto Rican family life is highly significant because it provides the physical and emotional sustenance that nourishes human relations and strengthens collective bonds. This experience has allowed me to rediscover and redefine the meaning of Eucharist, the Catholic ritual of thanksgiving in which bread and wine are shared. For me, this symbolic meal is an act of communal solidarity as we pass the cup and break the bread in recognition and affirmation of our ties to one another. In addition, in the Eucharist we celebrate the embodiment of our God. This embodiment is central to any discussion of spirituality coming from a woman who is defined, in part, by what she does with her body. Lastly, the Eucharist is a call to remember a crucified Savior. This remembrance re-calls us to struggle for a new world order in which God is present. These foci of Eucharistic symbolism have deeply affected my relationship with Christianity.

For Christians, Jesus Christ is God incarnate, God embodied, and as such, the Christ figure affirms the primacy of bodily life as the essential means to experience and express God. Whoever or whatever our God is will be manifested through our bodies. My vision of lovemaking as a way to experience God is not odd given this theology. My lovemaking is about God, just as love, in all its warm feelings, has always been identified with God. Despite the fact that within the Christian tradition woman has been defined by the physical pole of the mind/body split, it is clear that this false dichotomy is incongruous with the embodiment of God, an embodiment which ultimately discloses the sacredness of bodily love. This belief is one of the reasons that I continue to find grace around the communion table and hold to Christianity as a viable option.

The Eucharistic call to remembrance takes this theology even further. In the Incarnation, God identified with the plight of humanity, with the suffering of the poor and oppressed. New

Testament theology makes it quite clear that we can only serve God by serving our neighbors, love God by loving our neighbors, know God by knowing our neighbors. As a Puerto Rican lesbian this has special meaning to me. I see God in my experience of my people as they struggle to stop American companies from strip mining their land. I see God in Hispanics who come to this country — victims of American economic, military and political policies — only to be further victimized. I see God when women, especially lesbians, are raped because a man wants to show them how much of a woman they can be. In the daily colonization of my people I see my God raped of Her true identity and murdered. I see again the crucified Christ.

Coming out as a lesbian brought this home to me in very personal ways. I already knew that without just cause people treated others differently. The one new insight I experienced clearly was that all of the reasons and all of the ways people discriminated against me were the same. I was emotional, irrational and unnatural, an unruly minority who needed to reform so that the status quo could continue. This was true whether I was a loud-mouthed woman in my neighborhood, a Black Hispanic in a predominantly white academic institution or a lesbian in a straight crowd, Black Hispanic, or white. In every instance I was associated with the "other," the carnal, the irrational as compared to normal people who were always white, male, straight and upper middle class. I am oppressed by racist, sexist, heterosexist and classist social structures and political institutions. In the Eucharist I come face to face with my own suffering and the suffering of my people, but as we share the bread of life we claim the strength to continue struggling for our full humanity. Though in the face of the world powers the murdered Jesus was a symbol of defeat, for those oppressed by these powers, this murdered Jesus remains a symbol of hope.

This is not a new or unique view of the Eucharist, at least I hope it isn't. The only reason this interpretation can be seen as a particularly Hispanic, feminist, lesbian, economically oppressed view is because life on the underside has made the ritual of Eucharist more poignant for me. The violent images and the absurdity of hope which are the Christian tradition are not as alien or metaphysical for me as they might be for other Christians. Violence, poverty, racism, classism, sexism and homophobia are the realities of my life. Struggle and hope are also part of my life.

I am no longer a member of the Roman Catholic Church, though I am still a practicing Christian. In many ways being a Puerto Rican has always assumed a reference to Catholicism, whether this reference came through defining myself as Roman Catholic or by defining myself as the opposite of everything it represented (my conversion to Protestantism). Reclaiming my Catholic roots has given me a fuller understanding of who I am and a clearer vision of what one Catholic symbol and ritual can represent. The ritual of the Eucharist affords me an opportunity to hope and dream. I can regain my strength at the table and continue the struggle that Jesus fought and others continue fighting. I am reminded that the Spirit and I are in this together. The power is ours. "Este es mi cuerpo, antregado por ustedes..."[3]

1. This Is My Body.

2. In order to witness to this communal spirit I would like to thank my family with whom I developed the lines of thought here expressed: Carlos R.S. Alvarado, Amy J. Samonds, Julio Martinez, and Frances Melendez, and those who helped insure clear editing: Toni Almenares and Delbridge Narron.

3. "This is my body, broken for you..."

Intimate Bonds:
The Foundation of Spirituality

Joy Christi Przestwor

The more I grew in intimacy with women, the more I found myself and shaped my own spirituality. Through friendship and a deepened love with women I was able to leave behind the greater portion of the weight of Catholic guilt and the burden of oppressive doctrines. This coming out process was a gradual one, beginning in high school, and continuing to this day. On the table before me are snapshots of this passage, pictures of the women I love and who love me, women who have shaped and continue to shape my life.

Photo 1: Maureen posing in front of the campus entrance gate. I was a high school student and she was a nun. I took risks with Maureen, and in return, she offered me a friendship in which I could explore myself and grow emotionally. Although I was a bright student I knew little about the links between loving, liking, sexuality, and reproduction. I was disturbed by my attraction for women, and my lack of interest in discovering my attraction for men. My classmates talked about their boyfriends and I felt "left out." Maureen's friendship offered me a safe context in which to speak freely about all those feelings and sort out my confusing emotions. It was Maureen who comforted me when my mother was sick, when my confidence failed, when my difference frightened me. I don't know how I could have survived without the support she gave. In long afternoons, quiet evenings, and "wee" morning hours, we touched and talked. I was regenerated by our love, but also scared to death. I had no words to describe our friendship.

Photo 2: Anna in front of the library at Catholic University. The summers of my high school years were spent with almost three thousand religious women and men who were enrolled in various degree programs at the university. I worked on campus serving breakfast, lunch and dinner. Anna and I had seen one another many times as she passed through the food line and by my cash register. She was a delightful and engaging woman. The summer after high school graduation was a horrible time for me. I cried constantly, felt trapped in depression, and addicted to an endless round of masturbation and confession. My plans to enter the convent in the fall juxtaposed with indulging in awful, forbidden thoughts left me feeling like I was doing something good girls don't do. Guilt had chewed its way into the marrow of my bones. Knowing me for three summers allowed Anna to see my distress and ask what was wrong. My conflicts tumbled out because our trust had been established by sharing artistic interests, humor, and pleasure in simple things. She responded by opening my mind to aspects of sex, conscience and choice that I had never considered before. I began to see the difference between looking at the Church from a rule perspective — what you can and cannot do — and a human perspective. I understood that my anxiety was related to my entering a way of life in which sexuality would be absent — or so I thought.

Photo 3: A group of nuns, each wearing her distinctive habit, sitting on the lawn of Catholic University. Seeing their faces now I recall my search for the "right" community for me. The search, begun in junior high, took several years. I bought a directory of religious orders in the continental United States and analyzed each of them. I was trying to find a comfortable fit between my own personality and the spirit and style of the community. Looking back I realize that religious life attracted me because of the freedom it offered me to grow at my own pace. I finally whittled my choices down to three: the Adrian Dominicans, for their intellectual excellence and teaching commitments; the Sisters of St. Joseph of Rochester, New York, for their participatory governmental model and their "family" emphasis in community structure; and the Franciscans of Winona, Minnesota for their graciousness and artistic tendencies. In the end I entered the Adrian Dominicans respecting their spirit, and feeling at home with their values. I look closely at this photo and see some of my former sisters, women of wonderful power who still struggle with the tension of their own definitions within a male-defined community and institution. To this day they inspire me to keep in touch with my own spiritual power.

Photo 4: Maureen on a wintry morning just prior to her final religious vow. By this time I had entered the convent and had broken every institutional rule in order to develop our relationship. Our encounters were more difficult because of the requirements of our daily lives: the rounds of silence, prayer and work. Furtively, we met in classrooms, bathrooms, underground tunnels and abandoned corners. Guilt finally drove us apart and me to the confessional. I broke off our relationship in order to concentrate on my religious formation and my commitment to the community. I could no longer sustain the tension of two allegiances.

Photo 5: A community portrait. My eyes focus on Kathleen and Margaret, administrators who scolded and warned me against developing close friendships. They had the demanding jobs of guiding the congregation through the transformations of the sixties. One of the issues the community struggled with during those times was friendship between members. We read books on sexuality that emphasized compartmentalization of feelings — and in the midst of this I was trying to live out a celibate commitment. Kathleen and Margaret chastised me often but years later they admitted their feelings of tension between what they had absorbed from the male rules established for communities of women and their own inner feelings regarding relationships. Their apologies, although late in coming, were genuine.

Photo 6: Loretta and Karen working in the community garden. We were novices together and each of us became ingenious at finding times and places in which to meet. We got in lots of trouble as we created our own hideaways. We were never sexual, but we received the grace of intimacy in our female encounters — sharing poetry, dance, or a good tennis match. Even without physical touching I sensed that the strength of our friendships was a threat to our religious commitments. But I was also making an important discovery: the more I developed close relationships in our community, the more I was experiencing the humanness of spirituality, the more I felt the truth that God expected me to be fully human — that's all! I discovered that the more I grew in relation, the more spiritual I became. Simultaneous with this realization was my letting go of absolutes — I was learning to lead with my heart.

Photo 7: Estelle, Michelle and I standing with linked arms. What rough days this picture recalls. How did we survive that enormous transformation from silence to community, from hierarchy to collaboration, from secrecy to talking about our lives? I had been elected as the representative of the younger sisters in our community during this process of transformation, and I found myself in remarkable conversations, like asking Estelle, then age 74, how she experienced menopause in relation to her spirituality. Here we were, pushing questions about the fine day-to-day aspects of celibacy, community, authority, and here were women who had spent the vast majority of their lives adhering to rules and regulations. We found through our long, honest talks that we had much in common. Our linked arms tell the story of this remarkable passage and our discovery of freedom through sharing the humanness of our daily religious commitment. Again, it echoed ever stronger: God expected me to be fully human, NOT PERFECT, and in that authentic humanity was the core of true religious values.

Photo 8: A group of sophomore students at St. Mary's. These adolescents forced me to confront myself. They asked me about my friends, my commitments, my doubts, my dreams, and my values. Who was significant to me? Did I spend much time with Sister Anne? Was I homosexual? Had I been sexual with priests?

In my postulancy and novitiate I was warned that my friendships with women were too intimate; now my students were using a label — homosexual — a label I feared. Their perceptions caused me to retreat. I suffered from serious mental trauma as good and gay were diametrically opposed in my mind. I stopped having any type of sexual encounter for three years to prove to myself that I wasn't gay. I told myself that at heart I just enjoyed people, even though, uniquely enough, the people I enjoyed most were women.

Photo 9: Constance in her room pouring over her teacher's guides by the light of the noonday sun. After three years of celibacy I had proved my ''non-association'' with the homosexual label. I felt strong and clear about my personal identity and sexual wholeness. However the ever-present avenger guilt crept under the doorway again, this time sliding in from a different quarter. Constance and I had each made religious commitments and were concerned about the impact of our intimacy on those choices. During this time I began to wonder if religious life could sustain me. The familiar questions of celibacy, community, and commitment surfaced. Once more I tested my sexuality with a man. I was faced with the issue of whether or not religious life could be the context for my growth. I chose to take time to explore this question while undertaking a program of divinity studies at Harvard.

Photo 10: Patricia on a trail at Walden Pond. I remember the great relief I felt when I discovered Pat in my first weeks at divinity school. Pat was a nun who had been very involved in the changes of the post-Vatican II period. She knew the upheaval those changes effected on religious sisterhoods. When she became my counselor, I poured out my conflicts about sexuality — especially my discomfort in sexual relationships with men and what they lacked as compared with my relationships with women. Through her artful listening and persistent challenging of my own guilt cycles I reached the decision to leave religious life, a choice that had been evolving for several years. It was Pat who helped me step out of the mire of guilt and choose the freedom to explore my love for women. But at this point, I still resisted lesbian identity.

Photo 11: Charlotte holding out the balloons she bought for my birthday. I can scarcely look at her face without feeling a tug of sadness. She had been one of my high school students and over a period of seven years, we had visited and corresponded. Our friendship grew and changed. Sometimes we touched. Sometimes we almost touched. In my first summer in Cambridge we began to live together and our intimacy deepened. Older conflicts surfaced, particularly my refusal to call myself lesbian. I fought that identity and insisted on bisexuality. It took six months of counseling before I said, "I am a lesbian woman," and then traced my journey back through two decades of relationships. For three years Charlotte and I lived together and our love was abundant and strong. These years renewed my commitment to a spirituality based on the fullness of my own humanity. Our love-making was deeply set in wholeness and prayer. My experience of feminine spiritual imagery grew.

Photo 12: Mother and Aunt Ellen on Easter Sunday. I feel torn by grief and rage every time I look at this picture. What happened was this: Aunt Ellen filed for, and received a divorce. In our Catholic family, divorce was a grave taboo. The divorce generated a pain-filled distance between Mother and Ellen — even though they had been very close. The conflict between loving her sister and obeying Church rules has never been mended.

This situation is not unlike the consequences of my coming out to her. I am still struggling with her silence, and with her desire to love me as I am despite Church rules. I think about our difficult, fragmented relationship and feel rage against the many ways in which men's rules pit women against each other.

Photo 13: Marcia, Joan and Susan at the lesbian conference on spirituality and sexuality. In coming out I found my own voice and was not frightened. I became an activist in the Boston-Cambridge lesbian community, particularly around issues of sexuality and spirituality. I conducted workshops, planned conferences, and grew in personal wholeness. With these good friends I was learning a very simple truth: the more I am in touch with who I am, the more I love myself, the more spiritually dynamic and alive I am. With them I was reaffirming what I had known all along: wholeness as a human being consists in love for self and others; spirituality is ultimately about relationships.

Photo 14: Myself, leaning against the rail of the Golden Gate Bridge. I look at this face of forty years and see a lesbian woman who celebrates herself, who names herself as value builder and spiritual leader, a priest in her own realm. I see a woman who will be involved with women for the rest of her life, whose coming out will hopefully never end.

Peacefully I put away my photos in time to hug Laura coming in my door.

Before I Had A Name For God

Martha Courtot

Before I had a name for God She lived inside me. She visited me in the changing light and dark. She lived in the strong sunshine and in the shadow shapes moving across the slatted fences of my childhood ghetto.

Before I had a theology of God I felt the enormous vitality of the spirit-world around me. Mischievous and wild, spirits led me through a wilderness of substance and early flesh. Later I would call those spirits angels, and in flesh and blood children, my contemporaries, I would see the angel force shining.

Before I had a name for Lesbian, I was one. In my Aunt Thelma's desperate embrace of my three year old self, or in my mother's voice which entered me in terror and adoration, my lesbian self reveled. Nevertheless, this lesbian self has often found itself put to sleep while the rest of me went about living the life that seemed expected of me, as if the lesbian self were not important at all.

Before I had ever read the word pervert in the dictionary, or heard the word queer flung at some young and helpless victim, I knew somewhere there was a name for me, secret and unspoken. This knowledge went to bed with me at night, and slipped inside my sexual child fantasies, wrapping itself intricately around the imposed guilt and impending doom I heard from the sisters in black, the priests in their long ritual skirts.

My mother's roots were hillbilly and Protestant. She called herself "a heathern" (sic) in a self-deprecating way, to distinguish herself from her Catholic-propagandized children. My father, Irish and French, was Catholic, Catholic, Catholic. His family's rare visits to us were punctuated by the question, "Have you gone to Sunday Mass?" We always answered yes, although we were mostly lying. My mother and father loved each other very much, but their traditions and natures were

natural enemies. The war between Catholic and Protestant had a
certain vitality in my own worn-down living room. When my
father died in my tenth year the war moved doomfully toward
the center of my own spirit. To this day the battle continues: will
my mother's bitterness and life-denying take the day, or will my
father's "devil-may care have a good time and then confess it,"
finally win out.

I spent my childhood in terror of sin which led me to embrace
it. The nuns and priests whispered the words "impurity" and
"adultery" in such a seductive denial of the body, while my own
body whispered its urgent and insistent desires.

Sister Miriam was tall and beautiful, with an exquisite
vocabulary. Language, for me, had contained enormous power
from a very early age. My eyes followed Sister around the room,
my ears listening carefully for each unknown word to fall upon
my heart. How I would embrace it! Perhaps this is why her consistent cruelty to me was even more piercing, even more life-
changing. Every day for two years, in the third grade and again
in the fifth grade, Sister Miriam humiliated, tormented, and
degraded my little child self. Every morning at Mass I prayed to
God to let me faint so I could escape the daily torture, which
always came from a different direction, so that I was never
prepared for it. But God seemed to have deafened Himself to my
voice. Sister's beauty and cruelty married my stubbornness and
pride. The couple continues to struggle inside me, wanting either
to come to love each other finally, or to let one go.

The girl I loved in high school was smart and blonde. She was
also fragile, afraid of her feelings, and walked with a swagger-
ing, confident gait. How to explain this prototype of all women I
have loved since? Did I know then I could love only her, or
women who would resemble her in some important way? We
went to football games, we talked ideas endlessly and we
developed our own form of intellectual competition. We danced
with each other at hot, sweaty dances. And sometimes, in the
middle of the night at pajama parties, she would let me touch
her — touch her skin, hair, breasts, hands, fingers, thighs, even
the dark secret part.

We spent four years together in a Catholic girls' high school
arguing religion. She wanted to bring me back to the Church. By
this time, I had already abandoned it, coming to believe I would

never be a good Catholic because of my sexuality. My body was on fire in those years, my hunger for touch an imperative I could not deny.

In our senior year she began attending Mass every day. She never told me why, but I suspected she realized that we were not feeling "normal" feelings towards each other, and she needed to withdraw. I sat across from her in history class, watching the way her ink-stained fingers moved across the written page, wanting to feel those fingers on the back of my neck, curled safely up in my hand.

From the time I graduated from high school in 1959 until three years ago, I believed I was not Catholic. But every Easter a depression overtook me. I found it difficult to survive Spring without a Resurrection.

Through all my life changes, I experienced an absence inside me. Once, while I was traveling across the desert, God appeared to me in the dust and terror of the great wide spaces. It was not a friendly God, and certainly not Catholic. Another time, in a fire circle in the Adirondack Mountains I saw my friend's spirit rise five feet above her head, and then fall back with a terrible thump into her body. I felt this as a blow to my own insides. She came to me later and said, "I'm sorry. When I did that, I could no longer see your face, and was afraid." Without even speaking of the amazing experience she knew what had happened, and that it had hurt me, as well as astounded me. The God around the fire that night was in no way a Catholic God.

In a cave in Colorado, dark and safe, surrounded by mountains of snow, I beat my hands against the earth and mourned each loss in my life: my mother, my father, my grandmother; I pounded the earth as the grief moved through me like a terrible storm emptying me out. The God inside me was no Catholic God.

Before I had a name for God, She moved through me. In the Adirondack Mountains, away from men, that God grew into a Female Protector and provider of power. For a decade I dedicated my life to women and to the strengthening of my daughters. We made circles of power, each woman a Goddess, each woman assuming her power. God no longer walked through the world as male and oppressive. The Blessed Virgin moved out into the world, rented space in women's com-

munities, cut her hair short, learned to ride motorcycles and fix
her own car. She carried her baby in one arm and radical pam-
phlets in the other.

Language had muddled my experience of God early in life.
The Church had given me harsh words and beautiful ones. It
had twisted my most basic and human impulses into defiled and
perverted instincts. It also created in me, or tapped in me, a love
of Justice never to be lost. This love, this sensibility of an absolute Justice continues to inform my life and my choices. It
gives a structure to an ideal vision of a world in which each
human being would be valued. This imperative toward right
relation keeps me working on my own oppressive attitudes.

All the prayers I learned so young remain rooted under my
skin. *The Memorare* brings me comfort; the Hail Mary and Our
Father center me. When I caress my own, or another woman's
body my fingers seem to be praying also, so that finally there is a
joining of the prayers and my longing for substance, for body,
for an end to the long loneliness which has been my life.

I believe that mysteries carry us along, even when we resist
them. The communion mystery has lived inside me my entire
life. After I started going to Mass three years ago, I became
involved in a *Cursillo*, a special kind of retreat for renewal.
Standing in an open field watching a priest and minister con-
secrate their separate bread, I felt something inside me break. It
was a moment of absolute silence and wonder. I was shown in
this instant how it is that brokenness is the requirement for coming togther as community: that out of each person's brokenness
a whole is formed which heals.

I reentered the Church to find out what was gnawing at me
every Easter, and what that little Catholic child, so far down in
my psyche, was doing. There was no way to communicate with
this forsaken part of myself, except to give it a chance to come
closer, to see if we could be friends.

One Sunday morning, after many false starts, I opened the
door to a Catholic Church. Vatican II had gotten there before
me! Women no longer wore head pieces. The seats of the Church
were not the hard wooden pews I remembered, but plain
auditorium chairs. There were no statues, except for one huge
Christ hanging over the altar. Even this was different, for He did
not seem to hang in agony, but in triumph. The day I mustered
enough courage to receive communion, without confession, I

trusted myself to that God who had remained with me even when I thought She/He was lost to me. I took God inside me and was home.

Meanwhile, some of my lesbian friends I had the courage to tell were silent and brooding on the subject, and then judgmental. Why had I reentered the dangerous domain of the Father? Didn't I know that the Catholic Church is one of the major oppressors of women, teaching us to hate ourselves, to sacrifice ourselves until we are little more than ground up dust under the feet of husbands and priests? I was reminded of the Inquisition. I was reminded of the anti-semitism that Christianity, as practiced, had fostered for centuries. What about sexist language?

I could quarrel with nothing they said to me. The institution of the Church is indeed destructive to women. Its insidious machinations in the anti-abortion movement have helped to keep women from taking control of their bodies and their lives, and have helped to separate women from one another. The anti-Semitism which it spawned has done untold damage to past and present lives.

Nevertheless, I was speechless. Mute in the Mystery. I could not say how I knew all these things to be true, and yet had to open those doors every Sunday to find my way back to original light. It was a very lonely time for me. At Mass, surrounded by families who probably would have been shocked if they had known a lesbian was receiving communion with them, I was often overwhelmed by questions about why I was there. Yet, after communion, I felt a oneness, not only with the Spirit of God within me, but with the generations of people who had followed their simple and complex beliefs to this altar. I came to realize that the Catholic tradition in which I was raised had been given as a sacred gift to me and that I had an absolute right to the good it might have for me. I did not have to accept the misogyny of the male power structure, and I did not have to allow male language to keep me forever an outsider. The tradition of grace, of transformation, of sacramental power, was as female a tradition as I might find, no matter how it had been glossed over by male values. If the language was patriarchal, I could hear under it the throbbing of a female language of the Spirit. This belonged to me.

In this process, Christ's androgyny gave comfort, and eventually I could accept a loving Father who could provide me with a power I might need in the world. Just because it had seeped in under my skin when I was too young to say, "Well, what about Mother God?" did not mean it was not worthwhile. And I felt the Female Spirit inside me moving freely towards wholeness.

I still don't have any final answers. I struggle daily to maintain my place as a Catholic lesbian. The Church I attended for three years has not explicitly accepted me, but neither have they made any attempt to exclude me. I know that the Church continues to oppress women and girls. There will never be true Justice within the Church until women and girls are completely enfranchised through the priesthood, trained towards assertive action, and encouraged to fulfill their potential.

Because of these contradictions, there are times I cannot bear to attend Mass. At other times, I know the only sane thing for me to do is to go to Mass and receive communion. God the Mother and God the Father now live inside me in an integrated manner. She presides over all rituals, Solstices, birthdays, New Years, Equinoxes; She helps me open and close circles. She rises inside me when I need the power to rise, and far away I can always hear her dancing and singing, even when I am in my deepest sorrow places. She is my Witch-Self. She avenges me. She protects all of my daughters.

God the Father accompanies me to Mass. He helps me to find the God in humans, especially in men, whom I have been so separated from. He tells me it is all right to be strong, self-affirmed, independent from any group, male or female. He continues in me the mystery of grace and transformation.

Before I had a word for God, She moved inside me. The Catholic Church gave me many words, some of them brutalized me to the core of my being, and some of them gave me an opportunity for brilliant illuminations. I will never say, as some women do, that I am a "recovered Catholic." I know I will never recover from the deep imprint of Catholicism on my being. I know now that God is larger than the Church would have us believe, and that even humans are better than the Church implied. I will always be grateful for the spaces inside me that the Church provided names for: Justice, Struggle, Love. These values determine my life and my work. As a lesbian, Love is a great deal of what my life is about.

She dances and leaves silver footprints on the beach. He surrounds me with his large and comforting arms. Spirits of all sorts move in and out of my life. As a child, I called them angels, now I see that we are all angels of God, sacramental vessels. I know now I can never again deny any of my true selves: the lesbian and the Catholic are bound together, inextricably, as they grew together from infancy. Wherever one of them goes, the other must come also, transforming not only the lesbian and the Catholic, but the forbidden worlds in which each finds herself.

Before words, the Spirit is

After words, there is only a broken image
the tree wants to flourish
but the water leaks out of a cracked bowl

Out of this brokenness
I have called my Spirit to sing
Though my mouth was dry from wandering

And there was no rain.

Until a better silence
shall gather me all up again
I will practice   on and on
my own lonely exile song.

Blessed are Lesbians Who Open the Closet Door, They Will Change History

To open the closet door is to affirm publicly the intimate desires of our bodies for physical, emotional, intellectual and spiritual communion with women. This empowering affirmation springs from a sturdy faith in the sensibilities of our flesh, a faith strong enough to survive the onslaughts of heterosexism and homophobia. Each of us who has opened the closet door recognizes that coming out is made easier by lesbians who have gone before us, and that our own coming out will ease the process for lesbians yet to come. One by one we are changing history.

Josephine Anne

Carol Seajay

*The sun was on her shoulders. Skin brown and browning.
Sunwarmed. The sun glinting off the canoe and bouncing off the
waves. Blue bathing suit ties against her brown skin. The
muscles under her skin a ripple of movements following the pattern of her strokes. Over her shoulder I watched the shoreline,
the changing pattern of rock and trees, looking for moose
among the tall pines. Watching the loons land on the water and
take off, I held my breath when they dived, trying to last as long
as they did. A new, treasured, long-sought universe was all
around us but when she pointed to the bear cubs and their
mother on the shore, my eyes were on her shoulders, resting in
her motion there, companion to my own strokes. At mid-day she
put on a shirt to protect her back from the sun. Some kind of
relief in me. But she rolled up her sleeves and her browned arms
reached out of the blue cotton to hold the paddle so comfortably, paddling deeply, blade feathering neatly across the wind
to ready for the next stroke. Her dark hair curled into the nape
of her neck. We were fifteen and on a Girl Scout canoe trip to
the boundary waters of Canada.*

She went to the Catholic girls school. I went to public school.
I joined Girl Scouts so I could see her every week. The next year
we were both elected to the inter-troop council. Little by little we
achieved an almost daily connection, a regular life together. No
mean feat, given that we lived miles apart and went to different
schools.

Sometime in the middle of our junior year I told her my
heart's desire: to become a Carmelite nun. My father refused to
sign the papers that would have allowed me to enter the convent
at 16. I would try again at 18. She, too, it turned out, was going
to be a nun, but she was in less of a hurry. After high school or

even college was soon enough. A teaching order for little children. No one said so, but there was no imagining men in our lives; to become nuns was the only choice.

But by the end of that year there was one problem: try as I might, pray as I might, I could no longer imagine relinquishing her for all time. The world? Yes. Possessions? Freedom? Independence? Yes. But her? I didn't know how to say it, nor even how to think about it. If only she could find a calling for the cloister... *that* I knew how to pray for. Only one thing made this less terrifying: she didn't want to let me go, either.

In world history class in my public school we studied different religions — Judaism, Buddhism, Hinduism. We learned about the interconnected, diverging histories of Judaism and Christianity, and were presented with a historical perspective on the Protestant-Catholic split. I found myself again and again in confession: "Bless me father, for I have sinned. I've considered the possibility of other gods before God..."

"Go in peace, my child, there is no sin in wondering, only in believing."

Jo Anne had no such problems. In public school, they teach about the Spanish Inquisition; it wasn't mentioned in Catholic school. Jo Anne and I fought about it, our worst fight ever. It wasn't possible, she said. If it had happened it would be in her history books, too. We were uncomfortable about it for weeks, kept distant, in pain.

I visited, sometimes, with two adult women that I knew through Scouts. By then I had a driver's license, and they didn't seem to mind my stopping by if I was out in the evening with the car. I told them about the Spanish Inquisition, my text books and Jo Anne's, and the quarrel between us. They were Jewish. They said there were more evils even than that in the history of the Church and gave me books to read about pogroms, about the persecution of the Jews by the Church in the Middle Ages. One book said that the Vatican had known about the Holocaust, about the murder and torture of millions of Jews in Germany during the war, and let it go on just the same.

I lost my faith over it. If not my faith in some god, certainly my belief that I could turn my life over to the higher authority of a Mother Superior, the Pope and the Church, and trust them to guide me in God's will. Catholic school would have kept me from knowing. For the first time I was glad that my father refused to let me attend. I stopped even trying to go to confession.

She leaned against the fallen tree trunk, reached up to brush my hair out of my eyes and touched my face. Holding my eyes with hers she stroked my face again and very slowly drew my face toward her, closed her eyes and kissed me, lips to lips. She backed off a little, opened her eyes, met mine and asked, "Again?" I could only nod. This time I closed my eyes too and let her lips on mine be the entire world. I was startled when I felt the wetness of her tongue against my lips, but she didn't pull away. Without thinking, I opened my mouth to her, felt her tongue entering my mouth, tasting, testing inside my lips, finding my teeth, coming in deeper, until my own tongue met hers, tongue to tongue, a touch, a taste. A move forward, tips touching tips, then flat stretched over flat, sliding back for the feeling of that, then both moving forward again to meet. My tongue answering yes to questions asked in her tongue, until our hands pulled each other close, to hold, to demand, to want more. The fear settled in my belly, above the other sensation, below the kisses, below the certainty of yes. Yes. This. Whatever this is. And more. Another kiss. A deeper kiss. I held her in my arms with certainty for the first time. Yes. This was right. She backed up and looked at me. Eyes held my eyes. Certainty there, too. We both wanted this. And more. Whatever that might be. "I have to go," were her words after a blessed long eternity. "The Queen Mother serves dinner at six, regardless."

Not ready to go home, I drove over to see my two adult friends, hoping they would invite me to dinner. They had just bought a house together and Jo Anne and I had helped them move. They never said they were lesbians or asked if we were. It would have been improper. Over dishes, trying not to burst with the new reality of it, trying to tread lightly on our tacit restrictions, I casually said, "I spent the afternoon with Jo Anne." I answered the raised eyebrow with, "I got her to make more of a commitment to me today than she ever has before." Remembering the kisses, the promise in her touch, I spoke confidently, as if it wasn't me who had been terrified all along.

It was late when I finally went home. Mom woke from her doze on the couch as I came in. I remembered, as she sat blinking and trying to focus her eyes, that I had forgotten to call to say I wouldn't be there for dinner. She looked at me quizzically. Did I look different? Did it show? Could she tell?

"The Sheriff's Department called here about five," she said finally. "They wanted to know if your car had been abandoned."

I must have just stared though my mind was racing. Five o'clock? It must have been just as Jo Anne and I were beginning to...

"They said it was parked on a deserted stretch of road in Walker Township and that someone called in asking them to investigate."

"I was with Jo Anne!" I finally found something I dared say. "She wanted to get some leaf and bark samples for Nature Day with the Junior troops." Or at least that's what she'd told me when she said she wanted to go to the woods. "Can't two Girl Scouts go for a walk in the woods anymore? I thought this was a free country!" That bit I borrowed from Jo Anne's classic fight with her mother.

"I guessed it was something like that. But I started to worry when you didn't show up for dinner. Maybe I should have told them to go ahead and look around for you." The chill down my spine told me what would have happened if the deputies had come looking for us in the woods.

She shook her head, as if still not sure she was awake, said goodnight, hugged me, and trailed off down the hallway toward her room admonishing me not to stay up too late. I stared at her back, stunned that none of the possible hells had broken loose.

Having given up the idea of becoming a nun, I now wanted to go to the university up on the hill where recently I had started working afternoons in the bookstore. Jo Anne couldn't decide. She was becoming friends with the postulant who was teaching her science classes. That scared me. I didn't know why.

Sometimes we kissed. Sometimes we didn't. Sometimes we kissed and held and touched. I would touch her breasts and the fear would settle in my belly again. She would hold my waist, kiss me, ask me questions in her touch that I didn't know how to answer. The next day she would be angry, distant, would be busy the next weekend, would go camping with other girls or have someone else staying the night.

When I confided in my older friends, one said, "It will be easier when you live together," an idea that took root and grew in my mind. The bank had a special deal on silverware. If you deposited a certain amount of money, you could buy a place setting for a small fee. They gave you the first and eighth place setting free. By depositing my whole paycheck, I could just make the amount. I found dishes on sale and bought them as a surprise for our hope chest. I read the apartments-for-rent columns in the classifieds until I could imagine the perfect attic apartment in the student district. It had dormer windows and a nook where we would put our bed and another for a kitchen with a table for study and we could take turns working and going to school, or we could both work and save and then go to school together...

But she couldn't make up her mind. Sometimes she still wanted to be a nun. We didn't talk about the Inquisition anymore.

Jo Anne found the excuse to stop by our friend Patti's one day when she wasn't there. Her sister let us in and pointed us to her room so we could pick up the camping gear we'd come to borrow. We left with the gear...and a book called *We, Too, Must Love*. The cover was torn off. Jo Anne had been trying to get that book into her hands since she'd first seen it at Patti's months ago and the only thing scarier than getting the book was trying to figure out how to put it back on Patti's shelf before she missed it. It was about lesbians, a pulp novel that pleaded for acceptance and tolerance. Lesbians "couldn't help it" and were to be pitied. Lesbians ended up alcoholic or jumped off bridges, had two-week to three-month long relationships and the best hope was that by her late twenties or early thirties, one might give up her ideal of the dream girl and settle down with whoever might be available. I was ecstatic. Lesbians existed! Jo Anne was terrified. But at least, having held the book in our hands, we could talk about it now.

Lesbians! The novel made the point that gym teachers were sometimes lesbians. Was my gym teacher a lesbian? Mrs. Hinkley probably wasn't. My gym teacher from last year probably was! Jo Anne's gym teacher? We tried to imagine Sister Ellen Marie with another woman and exploded into giggles. Aha! Young single women who *weren't* nuns: my Scout troop advisor? Probably! She was thick with one of the counselors from camp last year and they had lived together for a while! Her Scout advisor? Not likely. (We were wrong, but that took a few more years to learn.) My adult friends? Of course! We went through the litany of every camp counselor we'd known over the last six years. Yes. No. Yes. Yes. Probably. We stopped to notice that we might be wrong about a lot of these women. We didn't care. We just wanted to wonder. Finally, we came to the real question: Us? Her? Me?

Me? Yes. If I'd had any questions before, I had no doubt now. But it was clear that I had to stay away from alcohol and cities with bridges!

Her? Yes. No. Maybe. She still wanted to be a nun, she thought. Could she be a lesbian and still be a nun? Could she make love with me and then be a nun? There was the postulant...but she wouldn't say whatever it was that she knew about the postulant.

We settled on one thing: we loved each other. In a rush I told her about the silverware and the dishes. We furnished the fantasy garret. Her mother knocked on the door and said dinner was ready. We went downstairs to our first exercise in closeting over her Mom's dinner of ground beef, canned peas and tater tots.

One night, while we were kissing she spoke in a hoarse whisper next to my ear, "I don't know if I can love you and still serve God," and she began to cry in my arms. I didn't know any answers, either. I could only hold her. But my next free day found me on the road to Mattawan, a town further away than I had ever driven before, to talk to the liberal priest there. It was Tuesday afternoon. He wasn't in the confessional, the only place I had met him before. I had to go to the door of the rectory and knock. He answered the door and I asked if I could talk to him. He showed me into his office, sat behind his desk and waited. Looking into his tired face above his clerical collar, jowls starting to sag, I wondered why Jo Anne trusted him so much. But I believed her trust. His eyes were kind. Looking into his face I made up stories about myself. Said I was my father's child from a time when he left his wife for a while, said my own mother had died, and that he had gone back to his wife, taking me to be raised by her. Adequate excuses, I thought, to justify my desires. I was just a poor unwanted orphan looking for love. Then I told him that the girl I loved wanted to become a nun. If we made love now, would they still accept her later, when it was time for her to go?

He looked at me for the longest time. And finally said, "Probably not, if they know what she has been doing." The emphasis was on "if they know." I couldn't think of a way they could not know. Weren't there entrance interviews? Wouldn't one have to be wholly honest about everything in order to be accepted? Wouldn't they be able to *tell* if you weren't? The questions must have been on my face as I got up to go.

"Pat?" he called to me as I reached the door. It took me a moment to realize that it was me he was talking to, for I certainly hadn't given him my real name. I turned. "One day you're going to have to take responsibility for your own life and leave your parents out of it, you know."

"Yes, Father," habit and duty responded.

"I'll pray for you," he offered.

"I'm okay, Father. Pray for her," and I closed the door behind me.

But I wasn't okay. How could I want her to make love with me if loving me would destroy her vocation? How could I put myself before God?

Jo Anne found another book: *The Well of Loneliness.* And then another pulp horror story. Each book frightened her more than the last. I didn't see what they had to do with us. She took to carrying them around school on top of her text books, as if daring anyone to say anything to her. She would walk into the Girl Scout office and set her books down in front of different staff members as she talked to them. Sometimes they didn't seem to notice. Sometimes they blushed. No one ever said anything.

One weekend while we were camping she left the books on top of her desk in her room. Did she do it on purpose? We were carrying her gear into her house when her mother came screaming down the stairs. Clothes and camping gear went flying in all directions as she grabbed Jo Anne and started shaking her and hitting her, screaming about perverts and queers and who was doing this to her! No daughter of hers was an abomination before God! She caught sight of me, a few steps behind Jo Anne, dropped Jo Anne on the steps and lit into me. A much bigger woman than I am, she had me out the door in seconds, screaming about court orders and getting a court injunction to order me to stay 300 yards away from her daughter at all times. Jo Anne was screaming for her father to come and make her mom stop. I landed in the grass off the side of the porch. She turned on Jo Anne again. She kept yelling about killing. I was trying to pull her off Jo Anne. Finally, crying, Jo Anne told me to go, that her mom wouldn't stop as long as I was around. I had to go.

Panicked, I drove to my adult friends' house, pushed open the door and just walked in, crying, terrified that Jo Anne's mother was killing her. Finally, sorting out my words, Betty put on her best Girl Scout professional voice and telephoned Jo Anne's house. Her mother answered. Jo Anne couldn't come to the phone. Betty asked for her younger sister and finally got Sandi on the phone. Was Jo Anne all right? She was in her room crying. Boy what a scene! Sandi had never *seen* her mother so angry. Was Jo Anne hurt? She'd have a couple of bruises, that's for sure. What had happened? Her mother found those books in Jo Anne's room, you know, those books of Jo Anne's? Right before we got there. What had stopped her? Her dad came home, finally. Sandi had called him at the shop to come and make her stop. Would she be at school tomorrow? Yep! Driven to and picked up afterwards. House arrest. No phone calls. No Girl Scouts. No nothing. She had to go. Click. Hang-up.

Jo Anne was alive. At least we knew she was alive. That was all that mattered at the moment.

But it wasn't all that mattered over the next few weeks. She didn't call me. Her mother wouldn't let my calls through. Once, she was allowed to the phone long enough to say, "Don't call. It only makes Mother angrier." I tried to find her at school, after school, but drove away when I saw her mother's car parked out front, waiting. Tried to talk to her in the cafeteria where we'd been so free before. "Leave me alone," she said out of a dead voice. "They're paying Sandi to spy on me. They've talked to the principal here. You can't come here anymore." And already the nun was walking across the room toward us.

"I'm trying to call you," she whispered, in a voice I could finally recognize as hers, before she turned and ran away. The nun, keeping silence, ushered me to the door.

She did call, finally. We talked when her mother eased up on her vigil a little and went back to her Legion of Mary meetings. Sometimes she skipped a class and called me on my day off. Sometimes I missed her calls and had to wait a week or more for her next opportunity. I could feel her changing. Could feel her

slipping away, her resistance to her mother, to hell and damnation, beginning to fail her. Sometimes it seemed she didn't even
try to call.

We met, finally, Good Friday afternoon while she was supposed to be in church. I parked my car behind the school, in the
St. Vincent de Paul thrift shop parking lot. It was rainy and cold
enough that our breath steamed the windows. But when I
reached to touch her hand, she pulled away.

What I had heard on the grapevine was true: she was going to
work for the summer in a Scout camp on the other side of the
state. She was fighting to be able to go to the university in town.
She could live in the dorm. But her mother was threatening to
cut off her college money if she didn't go to the Catholic college
in Detroit. Jo Anne was threatening not to go to college at all if
she couldn't go in town. Don't you see? We'll have so much
more freedom? I'll be in a dorm and they can't watch you
always in a college! A spark of herself returned.

But we don't need your college money! We can be together all
the time! We can live together, and work and go to school! We
can! We can do it!

Maybe you can, but I can't. It's too hard. I'm not smart
enough to do all that and make it through. Mother says it's too
hard to cook and clean and shop and laundry and all that. College by itself is hard enough. You want too much. You're being
selfish! Can't you see that?

She left. She was crying. I was crying. We never even broke
up, really.

Midsummer she called me from the camp. She was having
days off, could I come up? The postulant, the student teacher,
was there; she was taking a leave from the convent and maybe
was going to leave permanently. They spent special time
together, but she missed me so much. Could I come? Everyone
teased her because she talked about me so much.

I said I was having trouble with my car, that I was afraid to
drive it that far. It wasn't true. My adult friends, perhaps fear-
ing for my sanity or perhaps out of kindness, had invited me to
move in with them. The study became my room. I'd fallen in
love with one of them, the one who had called in the night to see
if Jo Anne was alive or dead. She wasn't undecided about if she
was a lesbian or not. She had no desires to be a nun or for
celibacy; nor did she promise to live in a dormitory away from

me for the next four years. And she was teaching me what my body was so hungry to know. I didn't go.

I stayed with Betty. Jo Anne came to the university, a school large enough that we didn't see each other for weeks on end. Sometimes one of us would catch sight of the other across a distance and just stand and watch. We met again in the peace movement three years later; she invited me to her garret to meet her husband. He was a little taller than me, thin like me, even his features resembled mine. He was heady, like me, unkind to her wiser emotions, and had all the character defects that I hope we have both left behind years ago. When his draft notice came, they fled to Sweden, the last home of the free. I finished college, then rode a motorcycle west to find a world with more lesbians and more freedom in it. I made it to San Francisco and stayed there, avoiding the bars and staying as far away from bridges as I could. She and her husband live in that distant land still. Her children speak Swedish and she dances. I do Tai Chi and have made my career in books, learning, as the years go by, what I can do to encourage stories about lesbians with endings other than alcohol, suicide and loneliness — and to create the books we need in the tender springs of our lives.

Coming Out, Coming Home

Jayne Young

For a while now I have been reflecting on the experience of coming out. In that process, accepting myself fully as a lesbian and becoming a Roman Catholic went hand in hand. How can a woman who was first a lesbian, then a feminist, and who still claims to be both, end up by becoming Catholic? The contradictions, on a superficial viewing, would seem insurmountable. I'm not going to attempt to answer all the questions here — partly because I don't have all the answers, partly because some are unanswerable. Looking back, I link the two together in the image of a journey: coming out and coming home.

Growing into my lesbianism was in some ways very easy. As naturally as a tree puts out leaves, I fell in love with women. The first time, however, the discovery of my feelings came as a shock. There was a sense of a predestined end to the relationship which would come about with the inevitable appearance of boyfriends as we "grew up." This short, poignant friendship helped me know a little more about myself, and behold, it was very good.

When I fell in love the next time — a love which has endured for seven years at full strength despite many vicissitudes — there were new matters to think about. The relationship opened my eyes to the politics of feminism, and to God.

God crept into it all. My living with Jackie, then a lapsed Catholic, meant that on many a long evening we discussed religion, spirituality and the Church. I took the part of the liberal agnostic — tolerating, almost pitying her views. I treated her faith as a form of incurable illness. She couldn't help it, but it wasn't really comprehensible. I would listen in an understanding manner whilst inwardly marvelling that any sane woman could believe that Jesus was God, and take notice of a church whose pronouncements were astounding in their arrogance and oppressiveness. I can't imagine how she put up with me.

As my knowledge of feminist theory deepened, so did my anger at the established order. Everything clicked into place. Everything I feared, suppressed and hid made sense. I knew *why* I was frightened to tell my parents about myself. However, unadulterated theory mixed with anger is a heady and dangerous mixture. It makes one take things out of context and forget the humanity of opponents. It gave me a lot of excuses to be selfish, hurtful and impatient. At the same time, this seemed right, for I thought I was being assertive, strong, and honest. Maybe it was a mixture of the two.

In any case, there is a still-potent horror in the memories of that time: the pregnant silence when homosexuality was mentioned on the t.v., the loaded questions, sidelong looks, the aggrieved air, and pointed comments favored by my mother before she officially "knew." The entire parental armory of disapproval was arrayed against me for months on end. Everything, that is, except an adult discussion. The messages were, "We know, but don't you dare tell us. If you tell us, we never even suspected." Under these circumstances the pattern of mutual misunderstanding was too well established for the final coming out scenario to run smoothly.

"I love Jackie, and we're lesbians." The magic words fit to be shouted and sung had to be uttered with dread. The family celebrated the happy union with a sort of prolonged collective nervous breakdown, congratulating me with frantic letters, stern manly talks and amazing variations of emotional blackmail. The very insanity of their reactions — the fact that I was forced to take them seriously — made me explosive with indignation.

Over a period of a year, I continued to visit my family regularly. I thought things would improve. In fact, every visit was a renewed test. I was asked to assume a burden of shame, failure and crime. I couldn't make even the slightest reference to my real life. Gradually, a sufficient amount of misunderstanding and resentment was laid by to ignite unexpectedly, but not inexplicably. It blew me and my family apart for the next two years.

I had always thought that coming out was a great and liberating experience. In fact, although I felt justified and righteous, I was also tortured almost constantly by remorse and guilt. I was ready to drop at any moment into a bottomless pit of sadness. I abstracted all the very best (or worst) reasons to maintain an implacable anger and threw them before the world like a skull and crossbones. I now see that I had a very simplistic idea of what coming out means. Much was lacking and still to be learned in order to remake myself.

The next part of the story is difficult to tell because it now seems so nebulous. It was more like putting down roots in the darkness than seeing the light. At this time, in my confusion, I felt the need to treat spirituality as central, rather than peripheral. It became a serious exploration for me. I read about the Goddess and welcomed the rich imagery of fertile chaos and the unending dance. Yes, that was like me. It seemed a long remove from cold Christianity, that ultra-cerebral patterning. These two spiritual paths, as I held them in my mind, seemed like a rich loam beneath a flawless vase: the first, an unexplained coherence; the second, a beautiful, austere artifact. The two revolved endlessly, both attracting and repelling me. The first offered a possibility of complete self-acceptance of all my feelings, including anger and pain; the second threatened to impose unwelcome concepts, like mutual forgiveness.

It was about this time that Jackie insisted on going to a group of Catholic lesbian women who were trying to tackle some of the issues facing them in the Church. I expected something a bit pious or a bit sad. It was neither. For the first time I was talking with women from all sides of the Catholic/Christian spectrum — some in, some out, some in-between — who were trying to respond to their faith intelligently, looking at the Church clear-sightedly, but without dismay. It was impressive.

Meanwhile, others of my loved friends were moving towards Witchcraft and calling themselves Hags. I found that very stirring, too. I wanted a way that was right for me, but something seemed missing. The truth was that I desperately needed to tune into something "outside" myself in order to bring my confused feelings into focus. I thought — or perhaps I only now see that I thought — that God was "outside" and could therefore be trusted to judge my situation with clarity. I required an absolute standard of love, a yardstick whereby my love for Jackie and my parents' lack of love for me would be shown up on a cosmic scale. That would be one in the eye for them was my general drift. I was toying with two sides of myself, still splitting them

up for clarity's sake, comfortable with the compartmentalization.

Gradually, the two images of spirituality began to spin. Out of
the whirling emerged Christ, the Young God, the Corn God. The
beautiful, impossible myth of a Creator totally and concretely
involved with Her creation suddenly became real to me. I
remember sitting up very late in the dark, listening to music
when a great excitement gripped me: possible, real Incarnation.
I whispered rather shamefacedly to Jackie as I crept into bed, "I
think I'm becoming a Christian."

I painted a picture of the Annunciation in thick, juicy oils,
moulding it with a palette knife. I thought, read, and had a go at
praying. I went to Mass, and felt the need and rightness of the
Eucharist ritual. Jackie and I spoke a great deal of the bodiliness
and sexuality of the Mass, the inside being bigger than the outside. I invoked God my Mother and Christ my Brother; it felt
full, fruitful, and delicious.

An awful responsibility disturbed my peace. I couldn't call
myself a Christian and take part in Communion while holding
myself in an attitude of hatred. The last thing in the world I
wanted to do was to face my family again; but that was the task
confronting me. The absolute standard of love I had invoked
stood before me in the form of the Christ; the standard had to be
applied to myself. I began to approach my problems with a
modicum of humility as well as self-justification. I found a few
gaping holes in my arguments. I saw where I had been lacking in
love. Suddenly, not through my agency, communication with
my parents was restored. Things were said which once were
unspeakable. There was renewed understanding on both sides.
Hard work still had to be done, but here was a beginning.

After this reconciliation, a few months passed in which I still
teetered on the brink of "joining" the Church. Of course,
many, many political objections stood in my way. These are
so numerous and so obvious — about Church structure, policy,
image, role in history — that I need hardly expand on them here.
What finally came through to me was that the Church was
not the monumental Vatican-based lump of patriarchy that I
loathed. It kept being said, but I took time to absorb it, that the
Church was *us*.

I watched my women friends *ashamed* of their religious needs,
trying to cauterize the wounds of involvement with their various

churches, each as destructive as the rest. Some reached into the darkness to find new ways to come to Christ, or to leave Christ behind. Some women made the decision to stick with the Church, because they refused to have their vision degraded by its context. Through these women I saw that the Sacraments are ours, meant for us. We are the community. We are the disciples. We are the wandering pilgrims. The message of God in the world, the Incarnation, speaks to us: women, lesbian and heterosexual, gay men, people of color, the poor everywhere. I saw the most radical challenge to patriarchy in the person of Christ. I felt the coherence of faith with my sisters — in *and* out of the Church — through time and space. I chose to accept with all women, my place in the Wilderness, for we believe that it is a good place to be: the place where you see God.

My reception into the Church was arranged through the Catholic Lesbian Sisterhood. My family, almost entirely secular in outlook, thought I was mad. Nonetheless, after a meeting of C.L.S. with the pew behind me ranged with lesbian women while one of their daughters served at the altar, I was received into the Church. Sister Liz, a sympathetic nun, gave me as a confirmation present a Madonna modelled of red, African earth, and a picture of the moon. On the back she had written, "May you be as full of blessings as the Moon is full."

Don't Look Back in Anger

Patt Saliba

Maronite Catholics are people of Lebanese or Syrian descent. The Maronite rite is similar to the Roman rite and we are under the Pope. Incense is used throughout the liturgy; the choir sings throughout the worship, and the Mass is celebrated in Syrian and Aramaic. It is one of the oldest rites of the Church and and is very patriarchal. Women are not permitted at the *bema* (altar stone) and are not allowed to become Eucharistic ministers. We are not modernized as the Romans are, and no one touches the Communion Sacrament.

Lebanese people are in reality Phoenicians. The culture is male dominated but not as stifling as some Arab cultures. Here in the U.S. women seem to be the dominating force in Lebanese society. Women in my community are strong-willed and seem to run their families as do the women in my immediate family circle. We are a clannish society and life centers around the church, the activites taking place there filling more of a social than a religious need. We have many festivals, *halfis* (parties), and get-togethers at the church hall. We are the only Maronite church in the Southwest and our community is very tightly knit. Many of the older people still have strong ties to the Old Country as they knew it before war became an everyday way of life as it is now. Naturally, there is intermarriage. Only a handful of young people have married others of our nationality, yet children learn the traditions even though only one parent is Lebanese. It is very interesting to see spouses from other ethnic backgrounds become "Lebanese" because they know they are marrying into a very old culture that values the language, the music, the food, and the church of their ancestors. This is how I feel. I have broken off now and then, but find myself going back. I am drawn by a need to keep my perspective on my race which is slowly dying out because of war. I do not feel religious, but I need to remember where I came from and the traditions which are my heritage. I have friends of many races and religions, but I like to remain close with my community.

My companion, Eve, and I have been together for nine years. She was a Roman Catholic nun but has since become a Maronite Catholic. Her association began one Sunday when I asked her to come with me to church because we were having a dinner after Mass and I wanted her to taste Lebanese food. She came, and a few weeks later came again. She liked the chanting of the priest, the way incense was used throughout the liturgy, the way we honor Mary, and the singing of the choir. After talking with our priest, she joined the church. She enjoys the fellowship of the community and has formed many friendships.

I have never experienced rejection in my ethnic community because of my lifestyle. I have never openly stood up and told them, "I'm gay and you'll have to accept me," because I am already accepted for who I am. My dress and mannerisms are what one might call butch, but I am never treated differently, nor is Eve, whom they have accepted.

In my family, it was a very different story, one fraught with pressures and trauma. When I was fourteen years old I came home one evening after a stop at the local hamburger stand with a friend. She was gay, very butch, but my parents had never said anything about her appearance before that night. She was five years older than me, but we were from the same neighborhood and hung around together. I respected her as an older role model, but we were so much alike that there was never any attraction to each other, simply a good friendship.

I will never forget what happened when I walked in the door. My mother yelled, "Where were you?"

"With Shannon, getting a burger," I yelled back.

She exploded, "I suppose she bought the food for you. She's your girlfriend, isn't she?"

The word "girlfriend" came out with a sob. She started screaming, crying, and yelling to my father (who was very calm) that "Patt is hanging around with those older queers. They're all so masculine; I know they're turning her that way."

I started fighting back with a vengeance. "Mom, Shannon is my buddy. I could never like her that way. You're right, they're all so masculine. Well, as you can see, so am I. They didn't turn me that way. I was born queer and I'll die queer. That's what you called me and that's what I am. And, if you're curious, *Diane* is my girlfriend; we're going steady.''

She responded with more fits of crying, laughing, and shouts of ''Where did we go wrong? It's against God's will.''

I felt guilt ridden, and scared that she was going to have a heart attack. She yelled to my dad for the phone book so that I could go to a psychiatrist. When I said I would not go, the crying fits began again. Okay, I'd go to a psychiatrist so life would be good again (for whom? certainly not for me). I'd do whatever she wanted just as long as she would stop crying and love me again.

That was a night I'll never forget.

The following day an appointment was made for me to see the psychiatrist. I was to see him for 30 minutes once a week. In our first meeting I was stubborn, refusing to answer him at all. I resented being there and I did not feel my life was any of his business. I sure as hell was not going to let him try to ''change me to normal,'' as I thought he was attempting to do. The next visits weren't so bad. I decided to answer his questions, hoping to bluff him, tell him I was okay, just going through a phase. But he surprised me by saying that he saw no problem with me; he felt my mother needed counseling so she could deal with my gayness. That was the last time I saw him. When he made this suggestion to my mom she said he wasn't any good.

Life went on in a way that might have driven others in my shoes to heavy drugs or suicide. I often thought of running away to Dallas or Houston, but my grandmother kept me strong. She was a feminist without ever knowing it. She taught me how to survive and how to find outlets for my anger when Mom's homophobia made conditions unbearable. Grandma never said, ''Patt, it's okay that you're gay,'' but she conveyed that she loved me, accepted me, and had faith that as I grew older I would be successful in whatever I chose to do. Her words of encouragement remain with me. I continue to feel her spirit telling me not to lose heart.

My mother and I never spoke of my lifestyle again. I was put on a heavily restricted schedule that left me depressed, but at the same time made me resourceful in finding ways to get out of the house. She listened in on my phone calls, opened my mail, quizzed me about every minute I spent away from home. She was obsessed with me and tried to instill in me the belief that I was going against the commandment to honor thy father and thy mother. So I learned to play her game. I went to a large high school and became friendly with many gay boys. Once in a while I would bring one of them home, and Mom thought I was at last turning straight. When I would leave on a "date," we would pick up our friends and have a good time going to the movies or football games.

I can't say much about my father's attitude towards me during this period. I never figured where he stood on the subject of my identity. His main concern seemed to be to appease my mother and, although I could talk with him about a range of topics, we never discussed my sexuality. I believe that he was uncertain how to handle it. To keep peace he sided with my mother, but deep down I felt he was mainly interested in my getting an education and trying to tone down the bitterness that was eating away at our household.

When I turned eighteen I went to my first gay bar and Mom found a telling book of matches in my room. After that, whenever I went to the bar I would get phone calls from her telling me that the police were going to pick up her and dad's car which she told them I had stolen. I finally said that I didn't need their car or their money; I would find my own way.

Even that did not appease her. I brought home gay women friends of different ethnic backgrounds, some masculine, some feminine, so that she might see that they were just ordinary people. Nothing worked. She condemned them. Life continued to be hell. I stayed away from my mother, got a job painting cars, and went to college. I was old enough to be out on my own, but guilt gnawed at me. I stayed at home, knowing that Lebanese Catholic women left home only if they were "married or buried." I was told that if I ever left home I would no longer be able to visit them, call them, or see any of the rest of the family, including Grandma. Those were the words that hurt, a threat that I believed and dreaded would be carried out; and I could never imagine myself without having a family to call or visit.

A year later I met Eve at a club. As corny as it might sound, I fell and fell hard. We started seeing each other constantly. I was interested in her recent past as a nun, but she steered the conversation to other areas. Weeks turned into months and I couldn't refuse when she asked me to move in with her. I had just gotten a new job in the accounting department of a medical lab only a block from her apartment. I told Mom I was moving in with a nice girl who lived close to my job. I don't think she had any more fight in her. I didn't want any more trouble. I felt that once I walked out that door I would lose my family forever, but I did it.

Eventually, Mom came around and accepted the fact that I was not going to be like her. She has changed her attitudes and is even fun to be around. I don't know if she has educated herself on gay experience, or if she just let time show her that I was only another ordinary person with the same wants and needs as anyone else. As for my father, he loves and accepts Eve as a second daughter. He will never admit in words that he has no problem with my lifestyle, but I already know how we stand in our relationship. I am proud of his inner strength.

I have had my peaks and valleys, but Eve and I have stuck together. When my grandmother passed away a few years ago I became ill with physical symptoms that could not be diagnosed. Finally, it was found that I had agoraphobia with anxiety attacks. I would experience intense vertigo and heart palpitations whenever I tried to leave home or have visitors. Through therapy I learned that my illness was due to my grandmother's death along with many other things that tie into my teenage years of being forced to stay home.

I have worked hard at recovery and am able to do many things again. I am not able to go into stores yet, or drive long distances alone. Presently, I am working with my brother who is teaching me word processing and computer technology. I also plan to work with my parents, but I know I will be comfortable around them now since we have all grown closer. I found myself questioning God's existence during the difficult years, but I have accepted that He does exist; that He created me, that He loves me. I still hold to some of my Catholic beliefs, but I know in my heart that my lifestyle is not going to condemn me to hell. Respecting others, helping those I can, and finding the good and beautiful in each person I encounter is important to me. No, I do not believe that God will damn me. I believe He's telling me it's okay to give my love to Eve. It's okay to follow the beat of my own drum.

Reaching for Integrity

Kathleen Meyer

When I left the silence and prayer of a thirty-day retreat in July, 1982 I felt deeply comforted by God's faithful love. Four months later I was caught again in the painful mire of acute anxiety and depression.

That predictable pattern seems so far removed from my present life. These last four years have been a time of healing change — changing faith, changing lifestyle, and changing commitments. What I realize now is that during the first forty years of my life I was sexually repressed, and that with the coming of sexual integrity I have found new spiritual wholeness. Let me backtrack.

My experiences of childhood in the forties, teen years at a Catholic girls' high school in the fifties, and novitiate training in the early sixties taught me to be good — a good girl, a good conservative Republican, a good nun. For years I was your typically good sister who said her prayers, trained altar boys and took high school seniors on retreats. In time, through involving high school students in Christian Service with oppressed people, I developed a broader world view and a political analysis, becoming somewhat of an activist.

I matured as a woman and professional person within the Church and my religious congregation. I was loved by my family and friends and respected for my commitment to justice work and education. Only my therapist and I knew that something was amiss. I experienced myself as painfully vulnerable and flawed and I didn't know why. Increasingly, I was emotionally distraught and I was losing all sense of self-worth. I didn't know why I cried, why my head pounded and my throat constricted when my counselor suggested I allow God to hold me and love me. I didn't know why I was unable to accept simple compliments. I was losing myself, and I didn't know why. Even the therapist, as helpful as she was, did not realistically address what I later realized was the main source of my anxiety and depression.

Three of five close female friendships I enjoyed over a period of twenty-two years had ended in disaster; two in considerable pain. The pattern was simple enough: a friendship would develop and in time we would realize that we loved each other. I would never feel guilty about my feelings for another woman, just careful to hide them from everyone else. In time, I would experience confusion over the tensions and problems that would arise for us, but we never talked about what was happening. Sexual feelings were not a subject for discussion, and certainly not feelings for another woman. After sometimes many years of friendship my unarticulated need for physical affection and contact with the one I loved would result in rejection and separation. Having been trained to think only about the dangers of heterosexual relationships, it never occurred to me that I was having lesbian experiences. I only knew/felt a deep emotional ache.

In the winter of 1983 I began to read the work of Catholic and Christian feminist theologians. It wasn't long before I too knew that patriarchal images of God were not meaningful to my woman's experience and understanding of the Sacred. I came to know God within me in an entirely new way, and "I loved her fiercely." I named God/ess as my Gentle and Faithful Source, whom I knew to have carried and guided me all my life.

In the following summer I was rocked by a powerful conversion; after so many years of personal alienation and slow disintegration I was converted to myself. A number of events led to that amazing moment. I had read *The Women's Room* and *The Color Purple* and felt deeply touched by the lesbian women in those novels. I identified with them so comfortably that I began to wonder if maybe I was lesbian. Soon afterwards I attended the National Assembly of Religious Women's Convention in Chicago and heard women speak out openly about oppression against lesbians and gay men. Because I was so interested in the subject I began to read *A Challenge To Love*, a compilation of articles about lesbians and gay men in the Church. The essays seemed to speak directly to me. One author declared that unless and until a large number of stable homosexual people shared their experiences, society would remain ignorant, frightened and homophobic. At that moment, I looked up from the book and announced to myself, "I am a stable woman, and God loves me as I am! I don't have to be afraid of my history any more." That was the moment of grace, the grace of integrity and courage to claim my own experience and lesbian identity. Yes, I had loved women all my life, and no, I didn't have to fear those memories any longer.

The months following that conversion experience were times of great personal joy and liberation. For the first time in my life I celebrated my being with generous self-affirmation. I felt good about myself — not the goodness that others expected of me, but the truth I felt within. Soon it became a matter of integrity for me to come out to my family, community, friends and co-workers. I refused to hide. The stranglehold of heterosexism was no longer going to control and destroy me. My mother and a couple of close friends had a hard time handling my revelation, but for the most part, people listened, tried to understand, and continued to love me. For many of them it was a matter of being willing to dismantle old prejudices and stereotypes and I understood this struggle because it was at the heart of my own liberation.

My political work and community life proceeded as usual but I soon acknowledged the need to look again at my vow of celibacy. When I entered the convent twenty years earlier I had not been interested in men or marriage. I had no sexual attractions at all so celibacy was an easy choice. I didn't realize that the particular friendships I had as a young postulant and novice might be a sign of homosexual orientation. In church and religious life people did not talk openly about lesbian experience. Compulsory heterosexist attitudes obscured the true nature of my feeling for other women, and precluded a necessary and sensible sexual education. Innocent as I was, I hadn't even heard the word "homosexual." In a healthier sexual atmosphere where I might have been free to consider that I loved women I might have decided I didn't have the commitment to live celibately in a community of women. At the very least, I would have been able to make a more informed choice for celibacy. Today I feel strongly about updating sexual education given to young people entering religious life. Directors should help candidates understand and accept without fear their own God-given sexual identity.

As the months went by a special woman came into my life. Lora and I had known each other and taught in the same school some years earlier. We had shared the same social justice orientation; she had marched with Cesar Chavez and worked briefly with the Catholic Worker community. Our friendship ripened into love and I knew I wanted to share my life with her. My experience of love, trust and intimacy with Lora was bringing me a blessed life and emotional wholeness. My feelings were signaling a new truth: what I needed now (what I had probably always needed) was intimacy for personal wholeness, no longer celibacy for mission. I was still deeply committed to effective action for economic and social justice, but I could no longer choose celibate community living. After twenty-three years in religious life I petitioned my community and Rome for a dispensation from my vows.

This momentous change of course in my life has borne abundant good. Lora and I, and our supportive friends, have been modeling something new in the Christian community. Soon after we had found a lovely place in which to live, fourteen friends came to bless our home with women's prayers and rituals. It was a day of celebration when they processed from room to room calling blessings and happiness on us and our life together. Since then our home has been a place where women come for hospitality, to worship, to reflect on changing and alternative spiritualities, to plan for justice activities, and to party and relax.

During the two years that I have been an openly lesbian woman I have been increasingly aware of the great silence about homosexuality that prevails in church and society, even among those who work tirelessly to dismantle systemic injustice. While many people are deeply committed to liberation struggles, few of those in religious circles work as eagerly against sexual repression of women or against the oppression of lesbians and gay men. Sexuality would seem to be a more personal, private issue than social or political. Even those who espouse wholeheartedly "the personal is political" often remain curiously uncommitted to a thoroughgoing critique of heterosexism — that "ism" which spawns the condemnation of homosexuals as well as sexist male domination, the use/abuse of women.

I am convinced that patriarchal heterosexism is at the core of every other systemic violence. The competitiveness, aggression, and domination that are the elements of sexism, racism, classism, ageism, etc. are first experienced in male-female relationships. Heterosexist prejudices are probably also responsible for the utter ignorance of some theological teaching about women and sexuality that has distorted the goodness of bodily experience and generated sexual fear and inhibitions for many people, whether single, married, lesbian, religious or lay. This is surely true of contemporary official teaching on sexual matters which blatantly denies and contradicts the experiences of many people. New creative thinking about sexual morality by those other than male, celibate church authorities, would do much to dismantle the structures that cause grief to gays and straights alike.

During this time I have experienced the reluctance of feminist women in the Catholic community to stand openly with their lesbian sisters, perhaps for fear of the stigma attached to homosexuality. Once again, heterosexism keeps women down — and apart. Religious and social prejudices, strictures and taboos against anything but female-male relationships are so thoroughly ingrained that they have been explored by relatively few justice-loving persons in the Catholic community. Silence, avoidance or even denial that this is a legitimate justice concern generally prevails. As a consequence multitudes of women (like myself for so many years) live in hiding and increasing alienation from themselves, their church, families and co-workers. We must seriously resist the institution of enforced heterosexuality and nourish the development of sexual ethics consistent with feminist insights.

Hopefully, as more of us stable homosexual people (and we are everywhere) tell our stories, homophobic myths and stereotypes will be dispelled. More people may then be encouraged to examine the distortions of heterosexist thinking not only in their own lives, but in prevailing moral and pastoral theologies and Church practices. Above all, at least a few people will better understand themselves and their sexual impulses and the potential for full, loving sexuality will be experienced by many more women and men. A new embodied spiritual integrity will be within reach of all of us.

I Request An Indult of Departure

Pat O'Donnell

In 1983, as I began the process of contributing to the then book-in-making, *Lesbian Nuns: Breaking Silence*, my concern was to assist others on their inner journey toward acceptance of being lesbian. From my own difficult and frightening journey I knew there was little published data to shed light on this area. I felt called to do my part. The interdependence of us all necessitates that we each contribute to the growth of the whole. This book was a fine way to reach out, I reflected, and I wanted to attempt to live the gospel message of liberation.

My ministry in spiritual direction via a holistic approach assists the other in naming and then claiming the inner aspects of Self. The claiming is done by honoring the revelation. I could honor my own lesbian gift in sharing my inner journey and at the same time give witness to the inner process that is my ministry.

The pain seemed to come from my own exposure of the sacred inner Self. I needed to get accustomed to this disclosure if indeed I was to facilitate others in exploring their own inner sanctum. Also, how else could I convey to persons who might be in need of an understanding Church representative that I had first hand credentials? One does not generally advertise her lesbianism!

As a Texas Dominican, I lived the Dominican Order's motto of *Veritas* (Truth) by sharing with the director of the retreat facility where I worked that I am gay. He seemed understanding. I was pleased. I knew I could not minister at any facility whose leadership was not open to my "who-ness."

In January of 1985 at the retreat center's weekly staff meeting I shared the reality of the pending book, that I was a contributor, and how important to me and others like me *Lesbian Nuns: Breaking Silence* would be.

I received the first copy of the book in late March of 1985 and promptly delivered it to the bishop of Tucson via the Chancery Office, along with a letter should the bishop desire to contact me. I never heard from the bishop. I also gave the retreat center's director a copy of the book.

In April, the *Arizona Daily Star* carried a very negative book review for *Lesbian Nuns: Breaking Silence*. Within the same section of the newspaper was another article written by the same reporter interviewing Church people regarding the book. None of the Church people had actually read the book, but each responded with displeasure. Was this not rather fear of the topic! Only the NOW representative spoke favorably and she had read the book.

From that moment on, at each weekly staff meeting, I was verbally attacked by five of the twelve staff members. One member requested that the staff be exorcised! Eventually such attacks got re-directed from me to the book and this seemed to satisfy the gang, in their Christian stance, that I would not be personally injured. So went each staff meeting of April and May. The other seven staff members were understanding but often fearful to verbalize their support openly.

Come the end of May, my contract deadline arrived. The retreat center director renewed it for the year 1985-1986. I was relieved! Honesty had been valued. My gift as a spiritual director and my own prayerfulness were being recognized.

The last Wednesday in June, this same director called me in to his office to announce to me my dismissal. On inquiring why, I was given such reasons as, "You've a cat and never got my permission to have it. You didn't help fold newsletters. You do not participate in the local community."

"But these are negotiable issues," I responded, "and you've never called me in to discuss them. Come on, the real reason is the book."

"Well, yes, some people have called and written — but they've requested to remain anonymous to you. Also, there is a fear that the center will become a gay place and be boycotted by straights."

"But most of the people I facilitate are straight. I didn't fold newsletters recently because I am doing the bookstore inventory. I've rarely missed any of the local community prayer events, have never missed a staff day nor a work session. I always eat with the staff and share in the conversation."

"So be it, you are dismissed."

I interpreted this as the chancery's long arm, publicly uninvolved, privately directing the action. Squelching is done in so many ways to keep the troops in line. How could I ever get another ministerial position in this diocese or any other?

I spent two weeks of July numb but knew I had to bounce back to life immediately in order to convince my own Texas Dominican leadership to give me permission to remain in Tucson where I was known for spiritual direction. I would seek employment in the private sector.

Yes, I found some groups of counselors open to a spiritual director, but no openings existed. If there was an opening, I did not have the capital to join the group. This left me with setting up my own practice and I had no capital to do that.

The Texas Dominican leadership, at my request to let the sisters of my congregation know of the book, gave input at three group summer retreats at our Motherhouse. People must have reacted — but not to me. On my short visit to the Motherhouse in July, four people spoke to me regarding lesbianism, but the membership as a whole seemed fearful of the topic. They needed time to digest this subject that had previously been unaddressed. It was this lack of verbalization of lesbian issues that had caused so much cloudiness in my own journey.

The leadership of the congregation was tense, too. No doubt they were under pressure and being questioned. Thus, at this crucial time I received little assistance in my adjustment. I felt it was a concession that I was given permission to try to set up a ministry source.

Archbishop Hickey of the Baltimore Diocese had written to the Galveston-Houston bishop forcefully suggesting that New Ways Ministry[1] not be allowed to give any workshops in the Galveston-Houston diocese. The bishop there complied by sending a copy of Hickey's letter, along with his own cover letter, to leadership in the diocese. This was my own congregation's diocesan location. The institutional Church wanted to continue to keep membership uninformed and ignorant.

Real personal help came from the lesbian/gay network and some straight friends — not only monetary assistance but affirmation, caring appreciation. These persons were living the community ideal. I realized more and more that church is people, not institution. I realized that the gospel message is indeed alive in society. I needed to live amidst such aliveness. The institutional aspect of Church was closed. I needed to accept fully the consequences of my "who-ness."

By November I knew I had to continue to inner journey. I had to speak out in order to live. I refused to be robbed of my "who-ness," or to participate in the silencing, the injustice against other gays and lesbians. I would request from Pope John Paul II disconnection from the institutional Church. In so doing, I could convey the basic issues, matters of conscience:

I request an Indult of Departure.[2]

I can no longer give obedience to a patriarchal leadership. It is oppressive.

I cannot accept the present teaching that the institutional Church demands I preach: It is okay for one to be lesbian/gay, but do not honor that God-given sexual orientation with expression. Only the heterosexual person can be free to make a choice of a committed relationship with another. This does not speak to me of natural law, nor God's message. I do not accept this directive.

I cannot condone U.S. bishops denying workshops within their diocese from New Ways Ministry. Keeping people in ignorance, demanding silence, prohibiting verbalization is intolerable to me. I see this as further oppression. It does not honor growth of conscious awareness nor a collection of data. Both are a must on my spiritual journey.

I cannot sit by and say "yes" to a patriarchal Church leadership that does not allow or encourage input from women. I do not accept clericalism.

The institutional Church responses to lesbians, gays and women are not compatible with my vision of being.

I request an Indult of Departure.

I continue to pray that this action will help the institutional Church to begin to grasp its rigidity, to see its fear, to look at its Shadow. I continue to pray for Mother Church that she can reclaim her nourishing qualities and diminish patriarchal power. In the meantime I accept my dispensation which took only seven weeks to receive. I remain a deeply spiritual person. I value my Catholic heritage. Because of this, I know my commitment is to God. I shall continue to honor God's gift of my "who-ness."

1. New Ways Ministry is a service of reconciliation and social justice for Catholic lesbian and gay people, their families, friends, and the larger Catholic community. It is located at 4012 29th Street, Mt. Rainier, MD 20712 (301) 277-5674.

2. Indult of Departure is a request by a religious who desires complete separation from her congregation. It results in a dispensation from vows and from all obligations arising from profession. The Prioress with the consent of her council submits the petition for the indult to the Holy See. The indult is valid and takes effect when the resulting papers sent from Rome are signed.

Blessed Are Lesbians Whose Eyes Are On Freedom, They Will Be Bold

Loving women engenders a love for freedom and the subsequent necessity to create a context in which lesbian existence can flourish. This passion for freedom appears as a radical act of faith in ourselves and a deep confidence in the meaning of woman-centered living. We lean into freedom out of an urgency made particularly acute by patriarchal violence. Our boldness rests on the faith that our love for women contains the power to transform and the conviction that as lesbian women we embody a critical message to the world.

An Open Road Before Me

M. Cunningham

I seek understanding for the simplest and most basic of human needs — self-preservation. Not to seek meaning would leave me only the empty meaninglessness of alcoholic despair. I have already known that despair in my life and it is remembrance of that awfulness that propels me down the path of seeking.

Born and raised in an Irish Catholic family during pre-Vatican II days I was imbued with the teachings of the Roman Catholic Church from the earliest age. Hopalong Cassidy and my Guardian Angel were the companions of my childhood. Never once in my early life did I question or rebel against the teachings of the Church; I found God via the avenue of dogma and doctrine. I said rosary after rosary, made First Friday devotions and dreamed of becoming a Maryknoll Missionary Sister. My dream was nearing fulfillment as I was accepted by the Order and happily planned on entering the convent the September after my high school graduation. At that point, however, the Fates/God intervened and changed my plans.

As a child of five I had held my father's hand as the breath of life slipped from his body; that summer after high school at age eighteen I watched my mother experience a slow, agonizing death. Orphaned and alone, I was devastated, and my understanding of God was shattered. To assuage my anger, intense fear, acute loneliness and utter fragmentation I proceeded unknowingly to drink the next thirteen years away. During that time I married my high school steady, graduated from college and graduate school, taught in Catholic and private schools, lived in five states, and advanced my alcoholic disease to extreme depths. Rarely did I ever step foot in a church during that time, nor did a prayer often cross my mind. On those few occasions that I prayed, I used the Agnostic's Prayer, "O God, if

there is a God, save my soul, if I have a soul." Oddly enough
even in the worst of my drunken despair I could never quite
bring myself to deny God completely. Finally at the end of that
drunken road, after six straight weeks of boozed out oblivion
and with a cocked .38 Smith & Wesson in my hand, I literally
cried out, "God help me."

My life has never again been the same.

With suicide only a trigger's pull away I had reached my bottom; I was physically, mentally and spiritually bankrupt. That
total and complete surrender to my helpless, hopeless condition
allowed something in me to cry out to something greater than me
for help. Somehow my agonized plea was answered and one day
at a time I began my recovery from active alcoholism. Slowly
my physical health began to return. Within a short time I had
stopped shaking, was eating regularly, and sleeping naturally.
(Along with getting rid of the bottle I learned my sleeping pills,
Valium, and cough medicine had to go too.) Mentally I began to
emerge from my alcoholic fog, although I was unaware of the
slowness of the process and always assumed I was mentally
sound. Spiritually I did not know which way to turn. Hesitantly,
at first, I returned to the Church and God of my childhood,
seeking my answers. Within a few years, with characteristic
compulsiveness, I had become associated with the Lay Third
Order of St. Francis and had begun preparation for my lay
vows.

But, again, all my planning was for naught. I read a slim little
volume of literature, and then followed it with another book
that altered my life forever.

It was an Ash Wednesday evening and I had settled down on
the living room couch for a comfortable night's reading. The
tiny little book had to be read before my next class and not being
naturally prone to reading outside of my discipline of history I
tried to make myself as comfortable as I could. My coffee cup
was full, the dogs were fed, the wood stove was full — there was
nothing else to fidget with so I picked up Virginia Woolf's *A
Room of One's Own* and began to read. I had not foreseen the
bolt of lightning waiting there among its pages but I heard the
thunder, the Click, when it hit me. Woolf named the illusion
that men and women walk under. I had never had a name for it
before. After finishing the book I wrote these quick thoughts,
"Why did it take me so long to read this? I feel almost a numb-

ness...can it be so?...but I know it is." I did not get off that couch a comfortable woman; rather in an instant I had become the classic "conflicted personality." On one hand a devout Roman Catholic and, on the other, a woman who had had her world view shattered by a profound feminist Click.

As if my personality and soul were not already in enough conflict, within a few months a friend of many years and I jointly read *The Color Purple*. She had come to visit my husband and me for several weeks' vacation and encouraged me to take a women's literature course which required Walker's novel. To my great horror, reading that fiction unlocked the ancient fear of my lesbianism and, even more horrifying, I realized I was in love with my friend and had been for years! She stayed for three months and, for the first half of her stay, I spent evenings on my knees pleading with God to "keep me pure in thought, word and deed." Again, as throughout the thirteen years of my marriage, I was terrified and disgusted by what I feared was my true sexual identity. Having been a deeply religious, guilt-ridden, twenty-three-year-old virgin at the time of my marriage I had anxiously awaited sexual fulfillment. Instead, for years I cried during intercourse, even though I loved the man I was with. He helped matters not at all by timing our sexual encounters and suggesting "dirty" books that I might read for arousal. Inevitably all of his books contained the necessary lesbian passage and to my unending horror it was only those sections that I found interesting. Then, one fateful July night, drunk out of my mind, I somehow ended up with an older, divorced woman. To my amazement, my husband shrugged it off because "it wasn't with a man." Unfortunately, I remembered just enough of that evening to be, on occasion, haunted by it in my sobriety. I had discussed my fears with a nun while on a Matt Talbot retreat. She flinched, pushed her chair back, and told me I was "neurotic" — an answer that quieted my fears for a number of years. On occasion, even my husband and I had discussed my fears and acknowledged that there was something vital missing in our marriage, a gap that even hard work couldn't resolve. Then dawned the sober realization that I was drawn to my woman friend of so many years. How was I to stay sober with these unwanted, disgusting feelings welling up inside me? I prayed.

I sat with my friend discussing the novel in front of the open doors of the wood stove. We both agreed that the depiction of love between Celie and Shug had been gentle and loving; then the wall that had separated us for so many years suddenly crumpled and we, two women, were in each other's arms. That cold October night in front of the open hearth I learned how beautiful lesbian love could be.

That awful, frightful, terrible word — lesbian — was me and there was to be no more denying and burying it. If I were to remain honest with myself and those around me, which I had to do to maintain my sobriety, I knew I had to accept my lesbianism. I, also, knew I had to share my terror and joy with someone, which I had never done beyond my one brief conversation on retreat years before. And so it was, several weeks later, that I found myself telling my fears to a lesbian couple. Even as I so uncharacteristically shared my experiences with those two women that chilly November afternoon I realized my lesbianism was a double-edged sword — it brought with it the joy and excitement of a new love and way of loving and the sad realization that the life and love I had shared with my husband of so many years soon would be ending. How fortunate I was that those two women acknowledged my pain and celebrated my newly recognized lesbianism. (Indeed, it was their use of the word "lesbian" — to the point of overkill — that acclimated my mind to the word.) As I drove away from the warmth and reassurance of their home I realized that, although I had honestly shared my experiences and felt a deep sense of peace in my sobriety, still, ahead of me, some painful, difficult decisions and radical changes would have to be made.

What I did not realize, thankfully, that November night was the depth of the emotional agony I would experience because of these changes in my life. (Supplemental to my extreme emotional and spiritual pain was acute physical distress leading to two D&C's and culminating in a complete hysterectomy.) Finally, I asked my husband for a separation. He countered by saying, "Why bother with a separation? Let's go for a divorce." The shock of his rebuttal left me reeling for two years. Here was the man I had loved for over twenty-three years, well over half my life, without knowing of my lesbianism, saying he wanted a divorce. Not only was my privileged heterosexual identity destroyed, but the security of my economic and social world was being ripped out from under me. In a very short time even my dog would be gone. In surviving these transformations I became aware that my childhood God was a conceptualization that I no longer felt was valid.

My lesbian feminism put me well beyond the walls of the Church and yet I could not condemn myself for I had been honest and truthful to the best of my ability. That God had been limited to a male symbol turned me even more firmly from Catholicism. Slowly, through substantial reading, I began to understand how patriarchy had controlled everything for thousands of years, including my own thinking. For some time I was nearly overcome by my rage at the violence of the fathers. I knew, however, that rage would get me drunk; I had to find a way beyond my rage. Where was I to turn for a faith to keep me whole? I began to see the Christ as a guide, Mary Daly notwithstanding. I responded to Jesus' words in the Gnostic Gospel of Thomas: "If you bring forth what is within you, what you bring forth will save you. If you do not bring forth what is within you, what you do not bring forth will destroy you." I had, however fearfully, brought forth what was me; I turned to myself and began to trust my awareness, my feelings, my knowing. Slowly, so very slowly, through unending days and nights of grief at my loss and fear of my unknown future, I began to understand and accept a God beyond my understanding.

My journey along the spiritual path, no matter how haltingly taken, led me to discover that Process of Evolution in the Cosmos is what I have always called God. It is the Presence, the Force, in the universe that is ever creating, ever evolving, ever changing. I came to glimpse that Process when I understood that just as the universe creates something out of nothing as it expands; just as I am part of that universe, even to the extent that the very atoms in me were present at the moment of Creation; therefore, I am a part of the Process and the Process is in me. I understand now that all life, all love is sacred because it shares in this Process. No church, no religion, no philosophy has the complete or only answer to explain this Process. Seeking meaning is an individual journey wherein the journey is the end result also.

Yet, even with this new understanding, my childhood indoctrination tore at me. Were not my thoughts paralleling those of the heretics? Had not thousands of women burned at the stake for questioning, confronting the Church? Was I in egotistical flight straight into the gates of hell? Hopalong Cassidy might have been gone from my life, but my Guardian Angel still dragged around ecclesiastical dictates. The angel could stay, but

the garbage had to go! Another crossroads in which I was forced
of necessity to trust my own truths.

Having firmly chosen to be faithful to my own unfolding, my
own being, I wanted to give my own lesbian feminist answers to
the questions that had always engaged my soul/spirit. Slowly I
realized that for me, personally, there may never again be outside answers, not even feminist theology may have the power to
control my journey. I cannot, having abandoned the woman-
hating Catholic Church, turn now, unquestioningly, to some
new doctrine. When I pray, how I pray, is my choice; I may
choose the words for the moment. I may pray to God or Lord or
Goddess as the need arises. I can pray to the Goddess, seek Her
presence in the women I know, see Her in the world/universe
around me. In turning to Her I believe that I am part of the mor-
phological process that is displacing male symbols which have,
for far too long, supported patriarchy. My soul/spirit/angel is
finally free to travel the road open before me.

Let me quickly and forcefully add, however, that freedom
does not imply security. Quite the contrary. My own spiritual
search has been a chaotic and painful to and fro, and I suspect
that other women seeking their own answers will encounter
similar dangers. From that moment of shocked numbness when
I agreed to a divorce, I was in a tailspin, caught in a spiral of
conflicting emotions. True, I had experienced the Click and accepted my own lesbianism and was deeply in love with a woman.
Yet it was just as true that I loved the man to whom I had been
married for so long; and I found this difficult to explain to other
lesbians. He and I had shared so many experiences, often we
thought the same thoughts. Then, too, as much as I hated to see
it in myself, part of my conflict came from the recognition that I
had a very comfortable and stable life with him. We owned our
own home, had two new cars, two lovable dogs, our own small
business, and money in the bank. Waves of paralyzing fear rolled
over me at the very thought of giving up the security that I worked so hard to achieve.

For many months I desperately tried to hold onto both truths,
to have it all, to juggle it so that I would not become like the Bag
Ladies I encountered with regularity. Even after I had gathered
the courage, out of the need to be honest, to tell him of my lesbian love I continued to hang on. To my relief he did not reject
me, nor condemn me. Unknowingly, he did something far

worse. He suggested I find another man "and make sure." After the house, the cars, the business, the money, and even the dogs were gone, I still clung to him for my definition/my being. Twice I visited him to see if anything could possibly be done to salvage my past dependency and illusions.

Finally, after two years of wailing and shivering in emotional pain, only one truth mattered: I am a lesbian. On that one truth the marriage was over and my past way of life was ended, beautiful illusions and all. Although many tearful, painful experiences still awaited me and await me now, I had survived; I had broken through to a new path. I had not found my way unaided, however. Throughout my fearful nights and tearful days my lover and friend had stood by me, held me, let me weep, and made me chicken soup. She had loved me with an open hand when I returned to him, and welcomed me with open arms when I returned to her. She gave me strength when I had none and awaited the outcome of my trauma; without her my journey would have been even more painful. She understood. Any woman seeking her own answers would do well to listen to Mary Daly's warning, "...the beginning of our rough Voyage...has proved — for those who have persisted — strange, difficult, unpredictable, terrifying, enraging, transforming, and encouraging." Freedom and authenticity allow no half measures.

Through all my experiences I've come to the startling realization that none of it matters, but all of it matters. The fact that I am leads me to believe that my reality, as I conceive it, is valid, that my thoughts, feelings, desires are all valid and right for me. I am, therefore, reconciled with my contradictions. I need not spend a lifetime trying to unify my personal paradoxes into a neat whole. I am a pacifist who loves guns, a feminist who works within the patriarchal system, a woman who seeks my own answers but wants everyone else to agree with them, and on and on. To be at peace I am learning to accept myself as I am while struggling to understand fully who I am. I must celebrate my life, my sobriety, my lesbianism, even my short legs. I am discovering that the joy of life may be had for the stopping and feeling. These "moments of being" constitute existence. The tender tone in my lover's voice asking if I want more coffee, the response of my body to the gentle caress of my lover's hand...and those rare moments when I feel a peace which surpasses understanding. Once and only once in just such a moment coupled with ecstasy I soared with an eagle over a desert mesa. I had no explanation then and have none now for why my mind did that, but I do know that I met that moment with all my contradictions still present within me. I have also known, once and only once, a moment of complete and devastating emptiness when I finished examining fearlessly my past wrongs. At that moment, too, all that was me was complete — contradictions and all. I am, therefore, acceptable to myself and in the Presence I shall go on unfolding.

Coming Out of Catholicism*
Julien Murphy

She who wants to save her life must lose the Church
—The author

Lesbians who seek to salvage Catholicism through some integration of their lesbianism with some notion of Catholic values are attempting the impossible. "Coming out" *as lesbian* entails a "coming out" *of Catholicism.*

There are three common ways of avoiding critical analysis of Catholicism: anti-historicism, romanticism, and Catholic humor. *Anti-historicism* involves a denial that the Church exists within a historical-political context, and a retreat into the ungrounded belief that there is a clear separation between the Church and the secular world. *Romanticism* appeals to a fondness for the Church fostered primarily by the familiarity of Catholicism. Our Catholic past is romanticized in fond memories of Catholic school days and Latin Masses. *Catholic humor* can be used to mask the reality of the Church in our lives and in the world. Catholic jokes require for their success an assumption of our passivity and degradation. Like anti-historicism and romanticism, Catholic humor is a powerful tool of political regression. I ask the reader, while offering no hope for indulgence, to resist these three sources of appeal and take up a critical stand for exploration of the real effects of the Church on our lives.

Lesbians must come out of Catholicism because the Church is a powerful and systematic source of anti-lesbianism in the world. To stay within the Church is to risk our own destruction. Throughout Christendom the Church has built a massive ideological structure of beliefs that attack the lesbian mind and body. These attacks are generated by the philosophical strategies upon which Catholicism is founded. Our recovery from these countless attacks requires a painful and courageous series of counteracts. The complete repossession of our minds and bodies requires a radical break from the Church.

The Church's anti-lesbian and anti-woman presence in the world affords no mercy for well-meaning Catholic lesbians. There is no way to rescue the Church without violating the connection between a lesbian and her sexuality — her very self. Any belief that a lesbian can insert herself into the Catholic hierarchy while insulating herself from its devastation is naive. Any belief that a lesbian can find a place within the Church that will safeguard her from being an instrument of the Church's anti-lesbian and anti-woman attacks is similarly naive.

The metaphysics of Catholicism splits up the being of Catholics into mind and body. The Church inherits this dualism from Platonism, which viewed a human being as a soul in a body. The soul was separable from and more valuable than the body. Roman Catholicism is founded in part on Plato's mind/body dualism, which both separates the being into mind and body, and prioritizes the mind over the body. In Catholicism, the soul is the most important aspect of a person. The soul is separable from the body at death and is eternal. The Church attacks the soul (mind) and the body in different ways.

The Church's attack on our lesbian minds begins at an early age, when we are told that our minds are not our own. Our minds are either the devil's workshop or the instrument of God. But not our own. Similarly, we are told that we lack the ability to discern truth from falsehood. The Church is the truth and censors our thoughts, books, and movies. Through the sacrament of confession, the Church makes an extreme violation of our privacy and personal autonomy a holy act. The sacrament of confession enables the Church to insert itself into the individual conscience of each Catholic. Through the practice of continual confession, we learn repeatedly to doubt our thoughts and actions and constantly to measure our motives against the Church's opinions. In the darkness of the confessional, inside an unlit Church, on Saturdays when others play loudly outside, we whisper the guilt and shame of our childhood "crimes." The activity of repeated self-censorship soon becomes an ingrained habit that prevents us from relating directly to our thoughts and feelings. What lesbian has not found it difficult to diminish the Church's thoughts in her mind in order that she may pursue her feelings of love for her friend? The Church brings its homophobia into the lesbian mind as it becomes the judge from within on lesbian sexuality. The goal of the Church is to be the divine interceptor, to make within each Catholic, at each occasion of sin, a self-constituted Inquisition. What if we were to stand in judgment on the acts of the Church? What would be our evaluation of the Inquisition? The silence of the Church as the Nazis exterminated millions of Jews? The papal Doctrine of Infallibility which alleges to remove all discussion of, and resistance to, the Church on its official policies?

Central to the Church's attack on the lesbian body is to see it as in the service of the soul. Hence, Catholicism has used bodily punishment to redress the offenses of the soul. Catholic bodies have undergone torture, fasting, flogging, hair-shirts, and martyrdom for the sake of purification of the soul. Catholic schools have used corporal punishment even when such practices have been banned in public schools. The Church has sanctioned specific acts of physical pain for "higher" ends. For what is the body? The Church declares that we are dust, "Remember man that you are dust and to dust you shall return." Dust is formless matter. The body of a person is as insignificant as dust. The insignificance of the body is demonstrated by the body's occasion with evil — the temptations of the flesh. The Church's view of the body as a hindrance to the soul, as the soul's torment, trivializes the most sacred of our lustful feelings: lesbian desire. The first step for a Catholic lesbian to "come out" requires an envisioning of her female body as beautiful and sensuous. Lesbianism requires that we first find our bodies.

The Church's elevation of our souls over our bodies results in body-denial and body-estrangement. We are taught not to live in our bodies, not to be at home in our flesh. As Catholics, we are estranged souls. To the extent that we take up a perspective on ourselves from above our bodies, or from outside our bodies, we are alienated from our bodies. Body alienation is inevitable if we are to sacrifice our bodies. For Paul, the body is a "living and holy sacrifice." He writes to the early Christians, "I urge you therefore, brethren, by the mercies of God, to present your bodies a living and holy sacrifice, acceptable to God, which is your spiritual service of worship" (Romans 12:1).[1] Catholic schools teach body-denial through nondescript school uniforms, heavy restrictions on speech, and strict bodily control. Catholic

girls are taught that our bodies are tabernacles of the Holy
Spirit. How can a girl's body be a tabernacle? And how could
one live inside a tabernacle?

Catholic girls are required to sacrifice the world of our bodies
according to an unnamed omnipresent Catholic fertility ethic.
The Catholic fertility ethic presents the bodies of Catholic girls
as bodies-to-be-sacrificed. The Church includes the bodies of *all*
girls in the Fertility Ethic, denying the existence of lesbians. A
Catholic lesbian grows up learning that her body is destined to
be heterosexual, and that *the body of every Catholic girl is
marked as the breeding ground for the Church.* The Church
takes for its mission in the world the complete control of sexuality through complete refusal to permit the control of reproduction (birth control). By maintaining one sexual practice,
heterosexuality, and denying all others, and by claiming that
(hetero)sex ought to be used only for birth, the Church achieves
its goal: birth without control which is materially equivalent to
"birth-out-of-control." This Catholic policy of birth-out-of-
control is the necessary underpinning for the covert Catholic fertility ethic, the most effective historical strategy for the subor-
dination of women and elimination of lesbians in the Western
world.

The fertility ethic mandates birth-out-of-control and its cor-
relate, women-under-control, by equating female *essence* with
fertility. The Church builds the fertility ethic from Hebrew scriptures which are a litany of female bodies birthing, and birthing
sons. We find the genesis of (hetero)sex linked with the genesis
of male rulers:

> Now the man had relations with his wife, Eve, and
> she conceived, and gave birth to Cain, and she said,
> "I have gotten a manchild with the help of the
> Lord." And again she gave birth to his brother
> Abel.
>
> Cain had relations with his wife and she conceived
> and gave birth to Enoch; and he built a city.
>
> And Lamech took to himself two wives,....And Adah
> gave birth to Jabal; he was the father of those who
> dwell in tents and have livestock.
>
> And Adam had relations with his wife again; and she

gave birth to a son and named him Seth.

And Seth, to him also a son was born.

(Genesis 4:1-26, *passim*)

Women's essence is primarily women's fertility. Although the Hebrew scriptures include prophetic visions of a virgin birth, the ideology of the fertility ethic does not culminate until the fulfillment of these visions in the New Testament. In the New Testament, with its emphasis on fertility miracles, particularly the virgin birth, the fertility ethic reigns supreme.

The "fullness of being" for women is the pregnant state. We are, supposedly, most with ourselves when we are with child. Mary is holy because of her conception, which is linked directly to the male child she produces, "Hail Mary, full of grace...Blessed is the fruit of your womb, Jesus" (Luke 1:42). The Church equates *female essence* with *fertility* through its two fertility heroines: Elizabeth and Mary. Both women are celebrated for fertility under unusual circumstances. Elizabeth is the *barren* woman who conceives, and Mary is the *virgin* who conceives. The women are relatives, and become pregnant at nearly the same time, both with sons.

The myth of the pregnant virgin sanctifies rape. Mary is raped by God, according to Catholic thought, because God impregnates her after first creating Mary without the ability to refuse his will, that is, without original sin. The fertility ethic teaches us that, like Mary, we do not own our female bodies.

The fertility ethic places women in a contradictory situation. It requires the sacrifice (rape) of our bodies, but declares that such sacrifice robs us of our integrity. Thomas Aquinas, a major Catholic philosopher of the thirteenth century, argued that all acts of fertility except spermless conceptions result in the loss of female integrity. Aquinas proclaimed that only in the state of innocence (The Garden of Eden) was coitus able to occur without a woman's loss of integrity:

> In that state [Innocence] intercourse would have been without prejudice to virginal integrity. For the semen could enter without the impairment of the genital organs, just as now the menstrual flow in a virgin does not impair her integrity.[2]

In a similarly contradictory manner, Aquinas portrays the broken hymen as the proof of our use of fertility, while at the same time it is the loss of our integrity. It is as if the virgin body is a sacred temple as long as it is unused (for fertility), with the hymen as the temple veil, and in coitus, which the Church demands of women, "the veil of the temple is torn in two from top to bottom," (Mark 15:38) rendering the female body profane. The loss of our integrity makes significant the breaking of hymen in the impregnation of a virgin. The Church has long exaggerated the hymen, using it in the twentieth century to warrant marital annulment.

The only acts of fertility that do not defile us are conceptions that do not break the hymen: conceptions in the state of innocence, and spermless births. Aquinas praised Christ for not being born according to a "seminal principle."[3] He debated whether sperm was a "surplus food" of the male body, deciding in the affirmative;[4] and he wildly speculated about a way in which coitus may have once occurred without penetration of the hymen.

In the Church's view of fertility, our essence is an inescapable evil. If we actually are fertile, our conceptions must be continuous. If infertile, we live in the guilt of failing our purpose. Either way we lose. We either drown in seminal fluid or drown in our guilt about our infertility. Our fertility plagues us. Such is the story told by John in Revelations 12:1-17. A pregnant woman painfully gives birth to a male child (Christ) in front of a waiting devil who will work to accomplish her ruin because she has given birth:

> And a great sign appeared in heaven, a woman clothed with the sun, and the moon under her feet, and on her head a crown of twelve stars; and she was with child; and she cried out being in labor and in pain to give birth...and the dragon stood before the woman...so that when she gave birth he might devour her child. And she gave birth to a son, a male child, who is to rule all the nations with a rod of iron and her child was caught up to God and to His Throne.

The woman flees into the wilderness chased by the dragon, has a temporary reprieve from danger while the dragon fights in the heavens with Michael and the angels, only for Michael to win, hurling the dragon back down to earth to pursue the woman once again. The dragon "persecuted the woman who gave birth to the male child." Rather than removing the woman to heaven for safety, God leaves her in the realm of the devil, helping her with temporary measures — two wings that "she might fly into the wilderness." Even with her wings, she barely escapes the dragon:

> The serpent poured out water like a river out of his mouth after the woman, so that he might cause her to be swept away with the flood...and the earth helped the woman, and the earth opened its mouth and drank up the river which the dragon poured out of his mouth. And the dragon was enraged with the woman and went off to make war with the rest of her offspring...

The battle of fertility in Revelations speaks of women's danger. The dragon's endless supply of seminal fluid pours out of him like a river, threatening to drown the woman in her fertility. God is polite but not merciful toward her. He gives her wings that cannot propel her high enough to safety. The earth, not the heavens, rescues her. With the Catholic fertility ethic, the nightmare in Revelations is reality for women everywhere who are in flight from the seminal dragons.

The danger of the fertility ethic is portrayed by the Church in modern times in familiar images of Catholic women dying on birthing tables. Since childbirth presents a serious threat to women's lives, an ethic requiring women to produce many children (big Catholic families) places women's lives in the greatest of peril. Catholic women confront their own death continually in the mandatory practice of fertility, the holy acts of uncontrolled coitus.

The danger of the fertility ethic also is portrayed in familiar images of Catholic women dying on abortion tables. Any woman who aborts in order to rescue her body from pregnancy is condemned by the Church. The Church continues to demand the prohibition of safe legal abortions in the United States and elsewhere. The Church fully intends its anti-abortion and anti-birth control positions to be legislated as policy worldwide. In this way, the Church attempts the material control of all women. Through the secular legislation of papal views, the Church has the means to control *all* women's bodies.

Lesbians can refuse to link our lives with our fertility. Our acts of passion do not include the impregnation of our bodies. Our sexuality is for ourselves, and not for necessary or continuous reproduction. We possess our bodies. Virginity is not significant, for lesbianism does not require acts of rape. With great vanity we own our sexuality. In this life, in this flesh, we seek our pleasures. And so, it is no surprise that lesbianism is a major threat to the Church: for the Church, lesbianism is an economic problem. Lesbians manifest a loss for the Church of reproductive members, since we need not choose to use our bodies to produce more Catholics. The Church loses actual wealth and political influence the more lesbians gain ground. Lesbians refuse the fertility ethic. We avoid its dangers, and we interrupt the birthing economy of Catholic women.

When confronted by the insurgency of lesbians, the Church acts to eliminate lesbianism. For as long as possible, the Church has hidden from us the lesbianism that gloriously resides in our bodies. Everything is done in Catholic education to suggest that our thoughts of passionate desire for each other do not exist. We are told that homosexuals are evil, that masturbation (the seeking of bodily pleasure without a man) is wrong. All avenues to sexual pleasure are closed off. We are told by the Vatican that we have "the right to choose freely one's state in life," but that there are only two choices, and both serve the Church: the family vocation or the religious vocation. Pope John XXIII writes, "Human beings have also the right to choose for themselves the kind of life which appeals to them: whether it is to found a family...or to enhance the priesthood or religious life."[5] Lesbianism is clearly not considered a vocation. Yet, against the odds, our lesbian bodies suddenly awaken. We find ourselves longing to touch each other. We begin our search for wholeness.

The Church refuses to name what we are. It chooses to omit the word "lesbian" and to classify us under the more general word, "homosexual." The Vatican discusses our "unnatural acts" or our "sex outside of procreation" or our "misuse of our bodily functions," but it does not mention "sex between women." The Church's silence on lesbianism as such continues a biblical tradition in which the only specific reference to lesbians is in Paul who refers to those "women who exchanged the natural function for that which is unnatural." According to Paul, lesbians as well as male homosexuals have "depraved minds" fitted to our "degrading passion" by which we "do those things that are not proper" (Romans 1:26).

The Church seeks to ordain our elimination through its denial of lesbian sexuality. By denying our sexuality, it hopes to produce such severe fragmentation within us that we can no longer exist. At present the Church appeals to a scholastic distinction between *being* and *acts* to condemn us. According to the Church, *being* a homosexual, which means having a homosexual orientation, need not be evil, since sexuality is a gift from God, and since sexual orientation is beyond our free will. *Being* a homosexual does not require homosexual *acts*. It is the latter that are truly evil and within the realm of our free will. The Church condemns only "practicing homosexuals," which is as ridiculous as speaking of "practicing humans." Our being and acts cannot be split, anymore than our humanity can be split into mind and body. For what is lesbianism without lesbian acts?

The absurdity of the distinction is revealed by an analogy to a thief. Consider making a distinction between the *being* of a thief and *acts* of theft, and then claiming that it is all right to be a thief but not all right to commit acts of theft. What is a thief who is innocent of all acts of theft?

The Church prohibits homosexuality by "tolerating" only non-practicing homosexuals. Homosexuality is confined to the privacy of one's heart for good Catholics. Homophobia is condoned not only in the world but within our flesh. If every homosexual abided by the Church's position on homosexuality, homosexuality would be eradicated from civilizations; for there would be no homosexuality unless people committed homosexual acts. It is only to the degree that we negate the Church's position on homosexuality that we can exist as lesbians.

For hundreds of years, the Church has harassed lesbians. In the early Church, Paul proclaimed that "homosexuals" could not inherit the kingdom of God, and that we were unrighteous, an untrustworthy people in the company of slanderers, murderers, thieves, drunkards, swindlers, fornicators and idolators (Romans 1:26). Thomas Aquinas provided sophisticated attacks against us in the Middle Ages that fortify the Church in its anti-lesbian position even in our own day. Aquinas decided that homosexuality was a sin of the gravest sort; a sin against nature. Homosexuality violated natural (heterosexual) law, and hence, homosexual acts were more evil than acts of rape, since rape was "only" a sin against human beings, while homosexuality was a sin against nature itself.[6] Aquinas went so far as to advocate torture and death for heretics, many of whom were judged "heretic" because of being homosexual:

> If false coiners or other felons are justly committed to death without delay by worldly princes, much more may heretics, from the moment that they are convicted, be not only excommunicated, but slain justly out of hand.[7]

Armed with the fertility ethic, the Church forces women into motherhood and marriage. Lesbians are left unnamed and under constant attack. Lesbians, with all women, are rejected from the ranks of Roman Catholic priesthood. We are coerced into the begetting of Catholic families or a celibate devotion to a male god. Yet, in spite of the Church, we continue to survive. For thousands of years we have endured attacks by the Catholic Church. In our Catholic childhood, we fasted our lesbian bodies so that we could perpetually make "communion" with a heterosexual Church. With bowed heads, under chapel veils we swallowed over and over "the body of Christ," and yet this sacramental act of oral intercourse between lesbians and the son of a male god has not obliterated our own sensibilities, our feelings, our lesbianism. It has never been the gospels that have spoken to us of our truth, but rather that special passage in Ruth that bespeaks our passion. Ruth clings to Naomi and says:

> Do not urge me to leave you or turn back from following you; for where you go, I will go, and where you lodge, I will lodge. Your people shall be my people, and your God, my God. Where you die, I will die, and there I will be buried.

> (Ruth 1:15-17)

What ritual can cleanse the Church of the tortures and deaths of the millions of innocents it has carried out throughout Christendom, and in our own day? What ceremony could cleanse the Church of women's blood shed by the Catholic crusades on women's bodies in the name of fertility? There exists no imaginable penance to absolve the Church from its most grievous faults committed not simply from moral fallibility, but from deliberaton and for specific political ends. The Church is a lesbian-hating and woman-hating ideological force in the world and has been throughout its history. The Church is a ruthless dictator disguised as an organized religion. It preaches Christian love and compassion while conducting widescale massacres of females.

Thus, a lesbian who seeks a safe place within the Church does so not only by relinquishing the rights of lesbians, but by relinquishing the rights of all women.

If a lesbian is to be true to herself she cannot have an allegiance to the Catholic Church; an allegiance to such a large and corrupt anti-female institution which provides us with only the most minimal sort of "DIGNITY." *Lesbians are not and have never been the Church.* The only way lesbians can recover from the attacks on our minds and bodies by the Church is to leave its ranks.

A lesbian may ignore the Church's political record in history and in our own day, and appeal to the solid values of Catholicism to justify her membership in the Church. She may value love, compassion and caring for others. But she must ask herself if the values of love, compassion, and caring for others are specifically Catholic values. I suggest that they are not. The only values specific to Catholicism are those that involve suppression of truth, intolerance of individuality, and control of sexuality. Thus, a lesbian need not be committed to Catholicism to hold the values of love, compassion and caring for others. Moreover, it would be contradictory to do so.

When we "come out" of Catholicism we recover our minds and discover that what is most dear to us the Church attacks. We find that we don't need the Church to decide the truth for us, to forgive us, to sanction our acts, or condemn us. When we have repossessed our minds, we can rejoin them with our bodies. Our lesbian sexuality provides the intimate connection between mind and body that dissolves the split. We become whole selves again. "Out" as lesbian and "out" of Catholicism we celebrate our lesbian lives outside of Ecclesiastes whose words ring loudly from all around:

> Enjoy life with the woman whom you love all the
> days of your fleeting life which God has given to you
> under the sun, for this is your reward in life, and in
> your toil in which you have labored under the sun.
>   (Ecclesiastes 9:9)

*I wish to express thanks to Jeffner Allen for her many helpful comments on this paper.

1. Biblical quotations are from the *New American Standard Bible* (La Habra: Foundation Press Publications, 1973).

2. Thomas Aquinas, *The Summa Theologica,* vol. 1, edited by Anton C. Pegis (New York: Random House, 1945), Q. 98, art. 2, p. 933.

3. Aquinas, Q. 119, art. 2, p. 1096.

4. Ibid.

5. John XXIII, "Pacem in Terris," in *The Papal Encyclicals, 1958-1981,* by Claudia Carlen Ihm (U.S.: McGraph Publishing Co., 1981), p. 109.

6. See Michael Ruse, "The Morality of Homosexuality," in *Philosophy and Sex*, edited by Robert Baker and Frederick Elliston (New York: Prometheus, 1984), pp. 370-373.

7. Aquinas, 2a, 2x, Q.11, art. 3, or see *The Inquisition,* G.G. Coulton (New York: McBride & Co., 1933), p. 37. For an account of homosexuals regarded as heretics in the Middle Ages see John Boswell, *Christianity, Social Tolerance, and Homosexuality* (Chicago: Chicago University Press, 1980).

Rosa's Letters to Her Sister

Mary Moran

October 1984

My dear sister:

I have wanted to write, but my life has been very chaotic ever since my visa expired.

Now I am working in the garment district of this city as a sewing machine operator. Me, with my education, who should be teaching. Oh Violeta, all I really want to do is to write, to speak freely. But as you know, without the proper papers freedom, even in this country, is limited. Still, it is more than in Argentina.

Let me tell you what it is like at my job. The room is filled with sewing machines, humming and clicking. No talking allowed. There are no motorized treadles driven by feet pressing down, pressing forward. No, these are the other industrial model, the one with the power handle hanging under the table. The outside of the right knee pushes the handle sideways. Legs spread open. Wider means faster, means greater productivity for the worker, greater profit for the factory owner. The knee aches. Thigh muscles tire. Until the leg numbs into the humming of the machine. Pre-cut patterns of sleeves and collars, shirt fronts and backs, carefully counted into bundles lay next to each woman's machine. Our fingers push and guide fabric pieces into the feeder feet. And in the end designer labels are sewn into the collars. Quotas of each woman's work are measured by the pattern count left piled at her place at the end of the day. The names of the fastest workers get posted on the bulletin board along with merit counts at the end of the week. Our sewing machines click out eight, nine, ten hour work days. And back at the loading dock, slower workers line-up and accept their bags of fabric to take home, to work into the night so they can meet the quota of the day, so they can keep their jobs.

There are other things, too, like what we women working together share. For example, Lucy and I started our jobs at the same time. We ate many lunches together before she told me how she felt bad about herself coming to work in the garment district instead of staying home to apprentice with Sabina. When I asked her who Sabina was and what she did, Lucy's face came alive with excitement. She proudly told me of this magnificent woman's life and work.

I remember her words: "Ah, Sabina Sanchez...You have not heard of her? We are from the same village in Mexico. When I was a young girl, I went every day to market so I could watch her do her work. She was there selling bread for her husband. He was a baker and that was his business. Her part was only to sell the bread. Her husband always allowed Sabina to do her own work...to embroider beautiful things on cloth. She did this every day, even as she sold the bread. Her fingers pulling the thread, gathering red, blue, and yellow into images of birds in flight...weaving vines that budded, then flowered like the rich gardens of our village. All this on the dresses, on the blouses she sewed for our women to wear at our fiestas when we dance and sing in the traditional ways. My dream was to learn, to study with Sabina. I wanted to continue her work. Do you understand? And I wanted to teach my daughters. It was important to me. But I married Manny. And yes, we had daughters: Maria, Elena, and Olivia. Then we came here. A job for Manny and a better life for us. Yet so far from home, from Sabina. As you can see, my husband lets me sew...here, on these machines. Oh Rosa, what am I to give my daughters now?"

I had no answer for her. I could say nothing. We simply embraced and quietly wept together. Then it was time to go back to work.

It is late and I am very tired. Please write and tell me how it is with you in New York.

With love,
Rosa

November 1984

My dear sister:

It is Sunday. I am at the beach, alone. Marguerite is hard at work to finish one of her housepainting jobs. My eyes close and I am in Argentina on our beach...I feel our sun warm on my skin...I hear our waves with my ears...You rub oil on your arms and legs...Mama unpacks the lunch basket...Aunt Eva frets as she watches our young ones play and swim in the ocean...My eyes open and I am in Los Angeles. You are in New York. Mama and the rest of our family in Argentina. I close my eyes again, but the dream is gone.

Last night I took Marguerite to an Argentine restaurant for dinner. Inside, very high class. Linen table cloths, crystal, silver, and fine chinaware. A single, discreet flower in a tall, thin vase placed on each table. Our waitress from Buenos Aires. And the food...Oh Violeta, it was heaven! Of course the price was high. Yet, we did not care. We ate and drank until our stomachs bulged. I grew fat with the foods of home. Marguerite was most gracious. All this, new to her. We talked of the differences of foods between our peoples. Hers is a combination of Ojibway and French-Canadian cooking. "Wild" meats and fine pastries, berries and nuts.

After our dinner, Marguerite and I went dancing at a club where it is approved for women to be together. Only women. We danced fast and wild — our bodies covered with sweat. We danced slow — our hearts beat as one. Only the language of music, of our eyes blazing for each other, of our bodies touching...coming together then dancing away and back together again.

All this led to our leaving the club and going back to Marguerite's apartment to spend the night together. Our passion for each other shared with ease.

Violeta, I truly love Marguerite. And she loves me. Yet, I know if I return to Argentina, she will not accompany me. If she goes back to Canada, I will not join her. We have talked of this, many times. It is a difficult, painful subject for both of us. For now, we struggle to live only for today and not worry about tomorrow. In our minds, we know we will not be together forever. The day will arrive when one or both of us decides to

end it by returning to our people and land. In our hearts we hope
and pray this day never happens. Sometimes I think we are
crazy, Marguerite and me. Fools-in-love, as they say, in a relationship doomed to end. Oh Violeta, what do you think about
all this? Tell me you will know my sadness and pain when
Marguerite and I end. Tell me you do not think me crazy for
following my heart.

With love,
Rosa

December 1984

My dear sister:

12 December, the Holy Day of Our Lady of Guadalupe.

Marguerite talked me into going to the events of the day with
her. At first, I moaned at the idea of it. Then agreed because I
wanted to be with her.

At dawn we assembled with the crowd at the church for the
procession. Half-asleep, my tired eyes were greeted by a banner
of Our Lady leading the march. *Mariachis* played *manaitas* to
the Virgin. The music and the procession of people a blur to me
at this early hour.

Celebration of the Holy Mass followed at six a.m. Inside the
church I admired decorations made of paper in the national colors of Mexico — red, green, and white. Marguerite told me the
children of the parish had made these "chains of friendship."
My nose filled with the smells of flower bouquets and burning
vigil light wax. During the Mass we exchanged roses and wishes
for peace. The roses shared as a special memory to the ones Our
Lady gave to Juan Diego at her appearance. When the woman
next to me handed me her rose, I thanked her in Spanish and
wished her love and beauty in her life. She wrapped her arms
around me in a big hug. My heart was touched. I held her close
for a moment, then thanked her again.

After the Mass, breakfast. The church hall rich with aromas
of Mexican food. There was coffee, *atole,* and *menudo* with
limes and *cilantro. Bunuelos* were served, too. We feasted.
Many people were dressed in colorful, traditional clothes of
their Mexican-Indian ancestors. My eyes delighted to see women

wearing *china poblana* style and men in their *charro* outfits. Conversation in Spanish heard from all tables.

The afternoon at Marguerite's apartment in the neighborhood was more celebration. We made love and then shared a siesta.

In the evening we went back to the church for the dancing. *Matachins* handsomely decorated with beadwork and feathers danced in their tradition as it was before the Spaniards invaded their people. Horns, violins, drums, and rattles played. My hand held Marguerite's tight as we watched.

What a day! I went to sleep that night and dreamed myself into more eating. Then, I became one of the dancers. Roses floated in the air all around me. Our Lady of Guadalupe was there, eating and dancing with us. A wild party, yes?! If I told mama of this dream, she'd be horrified and plead with me to see the priest at once. Such pleasure, a sign of the devil!! And dreaming of Our Lady as one of us, unthinkable heresy!!

I write to tell you this Holy Day was one of much beauty and strength for me. Of celebration and solidarity with Mexican-Indian people here. I wish you could have joined us.

                                                      With love,
                                                      Rosa

                                                      January 1985

My dear sister:

News of Maria Luisa Bromberg. Have you heard? *Camila* is nominated for the position of best foreign-language film of the year with the Academy Awards of Hollywood. Yes, it is the same Camila O'Gorman who eloped with that Jesuit during the time of De Rosa. This scandal of our country finally to be told.

I hear Bromberg brilliantly exposes the hypocrisy of the Catholic Church through the film. I cheer her!! They say she shows the dictatorship, violence, and abuse of power in the history of our country.

At sixty-two years of age she is a renegade, our Maria! Of making women the main character in her films, she has been quoted in the interview here as saying she wants to make images of us as "rich, contradictory, active...because I think passivity is the worst ingredient in a woman's identity." She says, too, that if she wins the award she will give it to Argentina, as a present to all of us. With highest pride as an Argentine woman I will attend the showing of *Camila.*

Since cultural censorship is less under Alfonsin and with this news of Bromberg's latest film, I think more of returning home. Always my dream to live and write freely in the land of our people. Perhaps now my stories against the Catholic Church might be published. But, writing of lesbians in Argentina...You and I know how the policy against that has not changed. I think this Alfonsin government is too new for me to risk return and exposure of my work. My fear is another military overthrow. And then if my identity and writings were known, I would become your sister, the disappeared one. Bromberg has placed herself in such a dangerous position with the making of her films. I do not have her courage, yet. I feel a certain safety here and I am writing my stories. But I cannot publish my work now because of my illegal status. Always something to complicate and control our lives.

I miss you, dear Violeta. Write soon.

With love,
Rosa

P.S. Sabato's *Nunca Mas.* Have you finished reading it? Tell me of your reaction to his account of "the disappearance." Does he expose the truth? our grief? our fear? our shame? How do you think his testimony compares to our mothers of Plaza de Mayo account?

February 1985

My dear sister:

A letter from Buenos Aires. My friend Estelita who I worked with at the university writes. She tells me of the digging up of the graves of our "disappeared ones" outside of the capital. The bodies exhumed and desecrated. I am horrified. They say it is to identify our dead. As if none of us knows. Who can forget any of the military dictatorship? Of seeing our friends and families taken away because they protested or were suspected of political resistance? We know the names of our dead. Yet, the government creates this diversion, this obsession now with grave digging. Estelita says a team of scientists from the U.S. has been flown to the medical school to examine the remains. They paw over the dental work in the jaws of skulls, count the bullet holes, bag and label each bit of hair or clothing. Fiends, all of them!

I am sick to think of Aunt Eva now. The awful wait for the day when she is called..."Come and pick up the skeleton of your daughter."

Do they really think that by giving us back our dead we will forget the murderers?!

Alfonsin promised us justice two years ago. Yet, who of the military presidents or members of the juntas has been brought to trial? Who of the lower officers, who did the actual killings, has been convicted? It is clear the military even now controls Alfonsin. And our fight for justice, far from over.

What is your reaction to this latest news from home?

I want to take the shovels from the hands of the grave diggers. Give those U.S. experts a one-way ticket back home. Rebury our dead ones, with respect. Then, get back to the business of demanding justice and trials for all of the murderers. But what use am I in this matter as long as I live in this country? Once again, I am pulled apart. Violeta, how do we live with it? Are we wrong to be here instead of at home now? When we left, it was so clear to me. We decided on life and agreed to return when it was safe. When has Argentina ever known safety? I feel mixed up in my thoughts and feelings again. I am exhausted.

Please write soon. I miss you so much right now.

With love,
Rosa

She's a Witch — Burn Her
(or, How I Survived Divinity School)

Mev Miller

> Seeing means that everything changes: the old identifica-
> tions and the old securities are gone. Therefore, the ethic
> emerging in the women's movement is not an ethic of
> prudence but one whose dominant theme is existential
> courage. This is the courage to see and to be in the face of
> nameless anxieties that surface when a woman begins to see
> through the masks of sexist society and to confront the hor-
> rifying fact of her own alienation from her authentic self.
> —Mary Daly, *Beyond God the Father*

At the end of high school (Catholic girls), I applied to enter
the convent. I wanted to do ministry, to be a disciple of Jesus.
The order suggested I reapply in a year but I never did because,
by that time, I was attending college and wanted to finish. I went
to a Catholic women's college and did a double major in English
Literature and Music History. Thinking seriously that I still
wanted to do some dimension of ministry, I volunteered at the
Campus Ministry. Mostly I played my guitar and sang for folk
Masses, but I did a variety of other things as well. When it got
close to graduation time, I panicked: I had applied to grad
schools though my desire to do ministry remained. However, I
didn't want to be a nun and couldn't be a priest.

At the last hour, I heard that the University of Detroit (a
Jesuit school) was looking for Campus Ministry interns to work
part-time while working on their Master's degree. I applied and,
two months later, I arrived in Detroit. After completing a
Master's degree in Religious Studies, I stayed on for three years as
a Campus Minister. During those three years, I became involved
in all aspects of ministry (without of course saying any magic
words), I volunteered with the Detroit *Catholic Worker* and

learned about the Catholic left, tax resistance, and anti-nuclear work. I came out as a lesbian and had my first lover. I became involved in the Women's Ordination Conference and started learning about feminism. I participated in the Theology in the Americas conference and learned about liberation theology. Although, emotionally and intellectually, these were the three most horrifying years of my life, I wouldn't trade them for anything. But I grew restless and decided that I needed to do more studying in order to be a better informed minister. I wanted additional theology and social studies, as well as practical experience to go along with the book learning. A Master's degree in Divinity seemed the most appropriate goal. Knowing that I was worn out from so many years of Catholic education, I decided to enlarge my perspective by going to an inter-denominational seminary. That's how I ended up at the Yale Divinity School. That was also the beginning of the end.

Perhaps my experience at the divinity school can best be described with an anecdote. One day I was standing in line in the cafeteria. I was wearing the button that says "Question Authority" and a male student in front of me turned and saw it. He said, "Well, that's not a very good attitude for a minister to have. How would people [meaning those being ministered to] react to something like that? You wouldn't want to give them any ideas." He was being serious. He apparently embraced the idea that ministers were always right and had total authority. I had a reputation at the divinity school for my outrage/ousness. Most of my energy went into questioning, dissenting, arguing, and challenging the beliefs and attitudes of my professors and peers. I was rebelling against *the* authority — not only of the Catholic hierarchy but also of Christianity in general. I was waging open war against the male god and his sidekick. Someone asked me once if it was because I was just angry at not being able to be ordained in the Catholic Church — you know: bad apples. It's possible, but as time went on it became clear to me that I didn't want to be a minister in a (hetero)sexist, misogynist Christian church.

In my first year at the div school I made some pretty clear decisions. I wanted to be out as a lesbian; I didn't feel like compromising that part of me. Besides, it was new and exciting. I sought out the lesbian and gay community at the div school and became involved in the gay/straight coalition. I wanted to be

more active as a feminist and develop my own feminist theory
and practice. I participated in the activities of the women's
center at the div school. As a lesbian woman, realizing I
wouldn't draw any real nourishment from the school community, I purposefully sought out the New Haven women's
center and endeavored to meet women and lesbians in the city.
For my field placement I worked part-time at the battered
women's shelter. I also joined the div school peace group and
with them did my first act of civil disobedience.

My experience at the divinity school was one of pushing at the
boundaries and digging at the foundation of all that had been in-
stilled in me in my Catholic life. As a woman and a lesbian, I
was already dispossessed by the Catholic Church in some major
ways. And though this was a source of pain and frustration, in-
advertently it created great freedom for me. Because the Church
authority essentially didn't care about me as a minister and
because I wasn't under the watchful eye of any bishop or Church
board, I could question and push and be noncomformist to my
heart's delight. I was antagonistic, anarchistic (anti-christic?).

Perhaps the key issue for me while at the divinity school was
the definition of ministry. My searching for understanding of
this question affected many of the decisions I was to make in the
following three years. Up until then, I had seen ministry in two
categories: 1) what nuns did — teach, coordinate CCD, hospital
work, running orphanages, etc., and 2) what priests did — ad-
minister sacraments, say Mass, run parishes, teach, run retreats,
etc. Growing up, the parish I belonged to was reputed to be one
of the most progressive in the diocese. I did see lay people
somewhat involved in church activities but not so as to make a
living from their work. It wasn't until I was a campus minister
that I began to see what role I, as a lay woman, could have in the
church.

My definition of ministry began shifting. I no longer thought
in terms of parish service but of active participation in the struggle to create justice. I became aware that the definitions of
ministry in the Catholic Church had to do not only with *what* ac-
tivties were considered as ministry but, more important, *who* did
them. Priests and nuns were divinely called to dedicate their lives
to the work of Christ. By implication the rest of us were only doing it on a part-time basis: we were just not committed enough
or there was some flaw in our spiritual lives. I began strongly to

resent and resist these attitudes, partially because I didn't want to be a nun and because I couldn't be a priest but I did feel called. Lay persons were instructed that our roles in church ministry were important but the hierarchy of authority led one to believe otherwise. In addition, my experience of the Catholic Church showed that ministry primarily attended to the maintenance and instruction of the spiritual community while giving less attention to structural injustices and pervasive human misery.[1] Ministering to the poor in spirit meant that the economically poor went unfed and unhoused. The most recognized ministeries in my experience were Mass, sacraments, prayer services and novenas, selling raffle tickets, and education. Doing community service involved an occasional visit to the hospital or convalescent home, the orphanage or mental institution — usually to sing Christmas carols. Our duty to the poor involved sticking money in an envelope to be sent to some food relief program or sponsoring a child in some far off place. The greatest act of charity, of course, was donating to the parish.

Ministry rarely meant empowerment. Politically, ministry was *to* someone which involved deciding what was best *for* them as well. Doing ministry thus became active to those passively being ministered to. This system provided a way of keeping the flock dependent and setting boundaries to the definition of power. Having certain persons primarily responsible for doing ministry meant that the rest of the community was not responsible for maintaining basic human rights and dignity. For those encountering injustices in their daily lives (women, people of color, the poor, etc.) being ministered to denied freedom and kept them praying for a future life when all would be well. In short, nuns and priests reinforced proper behavior in parishioners — to believe Church authorities unquestioningly and to do enough morally good so as to avoid hell. It was a pretty self-serving system meant to encourage passivity.

As a lay woman, forever to be so, I began to question these notions. What about the economically poor? How did my lifestyle affect the continuation of world poverty? Was nuclear production and weapons proliferation moral? How could the Church espouse the dignity of life but be so rigid and hateful toward women? How could homosexuality be innately sinful? (I never tortured myself about this — frankly, I just never believed it.) What about corporate crime and the evils of racism and anti-Semitism? Given the ministry of Jesus, how could the Catholic Church be so narrow about the meaning of Christian life? It seemed to me that the Catholic Church never took the biblical challenge seriously or appropriately enough. I had been brought up thinking that religion was a private thing not to be applied to our real lives. Justice went undone.

As a woman, lesbian, and layperson, it seemed that no matter what I did, no matter how noble, it would never be legitimate. I would only be believable if I was ordained or somehow affirmed by the "community." It was clear that as a woman I wouldn't have any valid authority within the Catholic Church. (I learned this as a kid — when I couldn't sing in the men and boys choir or be an altar boy.)

In my second year at the school, I became more outspoken and more of a visible threat. I was hired as one of the div school women's center coordinators, identified as the campus lesbian feminist, and I worked on the div school task force against racism and sexism (a group primarily advocating the hiring of women and people of color to the faculty). I was also outspoken on liberation theology and anti-nuclear issues, and was involved in the New Haven lesbian community through the women's center, the battered women's shelter board, the softball team, and the feminist union anti-nuclear task force. As a musician, I began performing women's music, especially my own. I was angry and belligerent. Questioning authority was a habit. I almost dropped out but wasn't quite ready to yet.

Traditional theology courses made me extremely anxious and angry. I took them as little as possible and only to fulfill certain requirements. In order to survive academically, I manipulated my course schedule carefully. This strategy included selecting "progressive" and sympathetic professors, negotiating specific class requirements, and creating interesting reading courses. I arranged my program to include liberation theology, social ethics and theory, religious art, and feminism. I read whatever feminist theology and theory I could manage to fit in. I was learning radical feminist politics and spirituality and encouraging other women to do the same. Fortunately, I was not totally alone as there were a few women and lesbian students and a couple of professors who were supportive of me and each other. I didn't study too much because I was always too busy. What I was learning in conversation and organization was more central to my sense of ministry. I insisted on my own empowerment.

Perhaps the single most debated issue at the div school at that time was sexist language referring both to humanity and to God in church services, music, theology books, and its usage by professors and students. Many arguments occurred around this issue clearly indicating the power of male-centered and dominated God language and its effect on women. At some point, though, I identified it as a non-issue. Christianity is a male religion which bolsters male identity through the recognition of a male god. No girls allowed. Viewing God as sexless spirit was a lie. This recognition made way for my final departure from the Christian tradition.

In Catholic tradition, the male god is maintained by a male hierarchy claiming absolute authority. I denied the authority and relevance of the hierarchy. I dissented from the power structure. I could no longer support a system of beliefs whose sole purpose was social control, especially of women. I would no longer be a sheep blindly following a shepherd. I would no longer accept the words or doctrines or statements of a bunch of men. What naturally followed, then, was my refusal to accept Christianity itself. I was tired of guilt and sin. I did not deny evil — there was enough of it around me to know that it existed. But I realized that I never, in my inner being, believed in the god I was taught to believe in. I only thought I did. Since I was a child, I had my own moral sense and indignation. What was being taught to me as "right" never really rang true. It wasn't until I became more acquainted with feminism and feminist spirituality, and recognized how I felt as a lesbian, and remembered all the injustices that I felt as a girl that it all started to fall into place for me.

My friends were clearly afraid of the direction I was taking. I was instructed to have faith. I publicly fought with a professor who frequently attacked me verbally. Students began ministering to me, seeing me as a sinner in need of being saved. I was repeatedly counselled. Suggestions ranged from praying, to having faith, to changing denominations, to not being so angry. One male student confessed to being afraid of the labrys I constantly wore. On the other hand, I was looked to when it came to rallying for certain causes. I was recognized as an outspoken feminist and expected to respond accordingly to every little thing. Most of the time, I thought I was crazy — or at least on the verge of a breakdown. But I was breaking the chains of thought and belief that had bound me for so long.

By the time I reached my third year, I was ready to withdraw completely. It was a year of survival. I could have dropped out but I needed only half a semester to finish. And I wanted to finish the degree partially because I was so close but also because it felt like I would be putting closure to my Christian life. I moved off campus, got a full-time job as an assistant manager in a bookstore, and went to classes part-time. I was becoming more comfortable with myself as a lesbian and as an ex-Catholic Christian. Essentially, I pulled out of the community life at the div school but I still wasn't finished with making statements or being present.

In my final year, there was no way I would identify myself as Catholic. In the student face book, I entered WICCA as my denomination. That proved to be the most startling action I ever could have taken. It created quite a hum. First, people didn't know what it meant and when it was clear it meant witch, panic spread. One friend told others it meant "Women In the Catholic Church Anonymously," while another friend told folks to think of me as Glenda, the good witch of the North. A follow-up action heightened the tension.

With a lesbian friend, I did a healing service during the regular chapel time. We moved it out of the chapel and created a space that was womb-like through darkness and candlelight. We prohibited all Catholic symbolism in the space and used non-biblical readings. We used goddess language and sang non-sexist and feminist songs. We encouraged active participation from those present and asked them to articulate in small groups what in them needed to be healed. We used scented oil to do anointing and allowed for whatever physical support people needed. Our intention was to allow for a multiplicity of individual religious expressions. The response was divided. Many women and some men claimed it was one of the most powerful and meaningful services they had experienced. Others felt insulted, attacked, and harmed. For weeks after that, I was accused of being a witch, practicing black magic, casting spells, consorting with the devil, and being the anti-christ. Now some of this may be true, but I sensed great danger for myself. I could have easily been burned at the stake if it was still allowed in 20th century USA.

In the end, I did graduate from the Yale Divinity School — greatly in debt but much more self possessed.

The resolution is quite simple. I am a radical lesbian and mostly separate feminist who was raised Catholic. I consider myself a deeply spiritual person but am unsure at this time how exactly to live that out. Reading the Tarot, using the *I Ching*, and deepening my felt connection with the cycles of the moon and the seasons strengthens my feminist spiritual path. I do miss a sense of community and the experience of ritual and celebration,2 but I am struggling to find some way of experiencing these in a new form.

The "ministry" that I sought so long to do is one that I am perfectly qualified to do. I do it in my political work — wherever and whenever I can. This work involves direct action, education, civil disobedience, discussion, analysis, interpretation, and music. My ministry involves a way of being in the world — my relationships, my style of living, and my work that I do for money. It is in my struggle to be consistent with the ethics that I knew instinctively as a child. It is in a sensibility that questions (hetero)sexism, injustice, racism, poverty, privilege, cruelty, war, and hatred. My spiritual journey is only just beginning but I can now say honestly that my spirituality is on the path on which it always should have been. Blessed Be.

---

1. This, of course, might have been more a function of class attitude and location rather than Catholic doctrine. There are communities of conscientized Catholics around the world committed to liberation in political and economic terms. The most notable examples include: the Solentiname communities in Nicaragua and other communities initiating liberation theology; the Catholic Worker movement formed by Dorothy Day; many inner city black parishes; the nuns who signed the Right to Choose document; and the Catholic left peace movement. These communities consist of faithful members and they exist *in spite of* the institutional church.

2. I believe that the Christian tradition has ripped off many matriarchal and goddess practices and symbols. I'm not looking to return to ancient goddess worship but to move forward into some recognition and connection with the goddess who is present in all women.

Mater Dolorosa!

Maggie Redding

For a long while my thoughts and feelings on motherhood were tinged with guilt and shame. When my own children were ten and fourteen I ran away to be a lesbian. I turned my back on the Church, too, because it had turned its back on me. But, since conventional wisdom, punitive attitudes of the people around me, and the consequences of my actions neither deterred me nor made me return, I learned to live creatively with myself, with motherhood and with the Church.

After all these years I still think of myself as having left my children. In fact, I left their father. For various reasons, including my attitude toward myself and their attitudes toward me, and practicalities like where would I live, and what would I eat, they stayed with him. He wouldn't leave. It was his house.

I love my children. I have learned to love them without possessing them. I wish Mother Church could learn to love her children in the same way. I feel in a position to criticize. They are in their twenties now and I hardly ever see them. This means that they hardly ever see me so are left to live and feed their knowledge of me from the myths and prejudice that blossomed in our family thirteen years ago. I had wanted four children when I married. I had three and two lived.

I brought them up very liberally. I studied them carefully and tried to supply their needs instantly. I presented food with love and I wondered where I had gone wrong if it was uneaten. I made sure they had sufficient sleep, abundant fresh air, companionship and freedom. I never complained about a mess; I welcomed hordes of children into the house and garden. I cooked (but didn't clean), scrimped and saved, took them on educational outings, introduced them to a wide variety of people. I hovered over them, looking for signs of jealousy — which never did occur between them. I thought it was because I had taken steps to prevent it. Although, because we were quite poor, they were not bought all the latest toys and clothes, I said and did everything I could think of to make them feel secure, wanted and loved. What they did have in the way of toys were sensibly chosen for their creativity — paints, pencils, crayons, paper, scissors, glue abounded in the house.

I was strict, in lots of ways. No being rude to people, no jumping on furniture, no destroying things. No fighting. And above all, "Love Daddy. He works hard." I was trying very hard to create a happy family atmosphere. In fact, what I created I shared, and other children, less fortunate for one reason or another, were often in the house, some staying weeks on end.

When it finally came time for me to leave, all of this "good mothering" made it easier. I had inculcated an independence in my children that I was proud to observe. There came a time when I felt they didn't need me, except to wash and iron and cook and clean. By this age, they were well able to amuse themselves, organize their lives, tidy up their messes. Daddy was more interesting than I was. I couldn't understand this. They flocked round him when he came in from work and I was left in the kitchen. Daddy this, Daddy that! I was becoming jealous. Why, my son wouldn't even allow me to pour a cup of tea for him — it tasted better when Daddy did it!

I began to find more interests outside the home, leaving Daddy babysitting. He didn't mind. They didn't mind. I didn't really mind.

I studied, I sang, I talked. I met people. I met women. Life was interesting.

Then, on July 17th, 1973 at about 5:30 p.m., the Truth struck me in a way I could not deny. It was a huge relief, the thing I feared finding out most about myself, the one thing I didn't want to be and had sat on for years: I was lesbian. Motherhood went to the walls for the next few months. Daddy could pour out as many cups of tea for both children for as long as he or they liked. I, for the first time, was interested in myself. It was like stumbling over the San Andreas Fault. The two halves of my life did not knit, did not belong to each other. But the chasm was overlaid by a veneer of marriage and motherhood. I felt cheated and lied to. I was angry with everyone for letting me get into this situation. I didn't want to be married, now that I knew. And I didn't want to have had children. How could a lesbian woman, I asked myself, have children.

Nine months later — a symbolic period — I left.

At first I still saw my children frequently and regularly. They seemed not to be suffering. Then after six months, things began to be difficult. Their father refused to allow them to travel to see me, although the journey, twenty miles from door to door, was easy and simple and then, soon enough, my daughter was suddenly traveling alone, some forty miles in the opposite direction, to stay with my sister. I held back my anxiety and tried to ride it out. I deserved such treatment, I felt, and somehow or other both children would be registering their protest. After the first Christmas away from my children (which I spent in the company of another lonely soul, a gay Catholic man), I didn't see my daughter again for six years. I knew nothing of her, what she was doing, how she was, how I had harmed her or not harmed her. She refused to see me, and the family — my parents, brother, sister — all closed around her father so that I could get very little information beyond the repeated, "She's all right."

My son continued to see me. Although it seemed to me that he was looking, at first, for goodies from his rich, young, free and wicked mother, I gave in to temptation only when I could afford it, which was not often. He seemed — and conversation with him was as difficult as pouring out a cup of tea for him — unconcerned by what I had done, only worried that he would be seen as a sissy going out with his mother so often. Sometimes I invited my lover's nephew to accompany us. This worked until they were about fourteen years old when class differences between them eroded the friendship. When he was sixteen, I saw the last of my son, except for a brief glimpse at eighteen. He had been in trouble with the police. I would have loved to have been able to help in a constructive way, but I did not learn of the incident until much later and only then because I had somehow guessed. Subtle badgering subsequently revealed some of the truth, followed by a painstaking search of the local newspapers. My son, from what I can gather, has settled down now. I only learn this from phone calls I make to him now and again which happen to coincide with his father's absence from the house. If Daddy is there, I get only monosyllabic answers, no sentences and no questions.

Seeing my son once a fortnight and, later, once a month was obviously not sufficient to challenge all the mothering skills which I had absorbed since a baby. So, within a year of leaving the family, I found myself back in the teaching profession, not just teaching, but having in my care pupils who had problems. I was good — I realized after two or three years. The pupils, mostly teenagers, liked me; I understood them and several of them I helped. Not only was the communication between myself and the pupils good, but I had means of encouraging them to do things other teachers could not. While some of these teachers disliked me openly, I tried to preserve a proper modesty and to avoid revealing my contempt for "the system" and the blind faith of its adherents. After my treatment by my family, I was fairly tough where rejection was concerned. I had developed a beautiful casing. No one knew my secrets, how I had left my children, that I was lesbian. I pretended I was a wonderful mother managing on my own.

Then I discovered I had breast cancer.

I saw this as a message from God. I rushed back to the Church. I forgave her for not knowing about lesbian women. I lay back in my hospital bed thinking that if this mutilating operation would bring my son and daughter back to me, it would be a worthwhile sacrifice. And I meant this.

The doctor asked me about my family. He thought it wasn't much to ask — just a visit. I was by this time living sixteen miles from them and the hospital was some eleven or twelve miles journey. I was sure I would see them. But they didn't come.

Once I knew my condition was not critical, I decided I had my life to live. And live it I did.

Having stared death in the face, I knew I had to grasp life fully, without fear. I started a group for Catholic lesbian women. I came out at work. I challenged the Church by speaking, nay, arguing with bishops, by writing letters and articles for Catholic publications. I appeared on television and radio. I said what I thought, and my thoughts developed. I lost all fear of authority and found my own. I lost contempt for myself and discovered a real contempt for the death-dealing institutional Church.

My lover and I parted. I moved some twenty miles further south to the other side of the city. I bought my own house and planned to share it with other women as lodgers. I vowed to live without a partner for two years, although by this time I was over forty. I was going to sort myself out. The second woman, also

Catholic, who came to live with me fell madly in love with me and I with her. She had left two children. I told her not to do it, there must be other ways. But she did it. And six months later, her nine-year-old daughter joined us. All my training in motherhood, all my guilt was promptly resurrected. A second chance! I can do it all properly this time, with no interfering man!

I knew so much more about children by now and I wanted to practice my skills and insights in my own home. And I wanted to save my lover from the agonies I had been through. Besides, the nine-year-old was a nice child.

At about this time, my daughter decided to come back into my life. She was twenty-two, and planning travels around the world. She wanted to come and see me and to see my new house.

What a shock she had. Whatever changes she may have hoped for, I was still a lesbian and now she had not only me to contend with but my lover and her daughter, as well. And I was a stranger. Yet after a few months she decided she would like to move to the big city too, and she moved in with us. For a while it was a comfortable-seeming arrangement — two mothers and their daughters. But my daughter was living with three complete strangers. She kept trying to relate to me as I had been ten years earlier and one day she just disappeared and went back to Daddy. The family grapevine some months later reported that she had left "Well, because, I presume, she couldn't stand the way you treated her." What every lesbian mother wants to hear, that sort of castigating phrase with its horrible undertones.

Meanwhile, my lover's daughter was settling in well. I threw all hopes of promotion to the winds, and rushed home every evening to look after her after school. I gladly took her on during school holidays while her mother was at work. I loved cooking for her — she ate everything. I gave her the best bedroom in the house and generally made a fuss over her. Unfortunately, so did her father, keeping her on access visits, threatening and promising to have her back to live with him. Court actions of one sort or another were mentioned from time to time and I was warned by my lover's lawyer that I might lose my job and therefore my home if any of this became public. I said, "Go ahead." She was a nice child and worth it.

Then one day, my lover went to see a lawyer to find out how to claim her financial share of the marital home from her ex-husband. The lawyer warned that her husband's retaliation would be to go for divorce *and* custody. And we all know the likely outcome of lesbian mothers' custody cases, if opposed.

The very same week of my lover's visit to the lawyer, a nine-year-old girl at school confided in me that she was being interfered with by her father. I made the appropriate report but neither I nor the girl was believed. Headmaster and psychologist were both male and took pity on the girl's father because of this "unjust accusation." Both parents accused me of putting ideas into their daughter's head. They all said the girl was fantasizing and it was all the mother's fault. So, at the same time that I was made aware that my lover's daughter could be taken from us because, as lesbians, we were not trustworthy to raise her, I was the only party interested in the fate of this other young girl in a heterosexual household who was *really* in trouble.

"Leave the money," I said to my lover. "I'll give up my job, I'll sell my house and we'll move somewhere cheap, healthy and beautiful, like Wales."

I was so angry, so beside myself with rage I could no longer participate in a society where women are the scapegoat for men.

So we opted out, tried to run away. We bought an acre and a half of land. And now my lover's child is an adolescent who yells, "I hate you," from across the garden, making full use of the freedom we've given her. "You took my mother away."

We gave her freedom to challenge us that no man would allow her. Yet she is faithful to Daddy, who tells her I took her mother away.

Last time she saw him he asked her if I ever put my arm around her and cuddled her. She was shocked, she said, because I had predicted that such a question would be asked. "Well," he had said, "just watch out for her. Don't get too friendly with her."

Aren't men wonderful, I thought and picked up the phone to discuss it with her father. He denied it.

She looked at me with new respect and wide eyes. "Why did he deny it?" she asked.

Motherhood would be so much easier without fatherhood! Do I believe in the Virgin Birth? I wish I could!

Loving Well Means Doing Justice

Mary E. Hunt

It is no secret that many Catholic lesbian feminists are involved in social justice work. Nor is it any surprise that many women who work against apartheid in South Africa and U.S. intervention in Central America, women who provide shelter for battered women and medical care for the poor are Catholic lesbian feminists. What remains unexplored and unarticulated is why this is the case. How can we encourage each other to continue in our work, as well as invite others to join us? How can we share how meaningful our starting point in concrete love and care for other women is in what motivates us to make change? I believe that loving well as lesbian women in a heterosexist, patriarchal church and society compels us to work for justice and, at the same time, that working for justice leads us to love well.

To be a Catholic lesbian feminist is, for many people, to live with an intolerable degree of contradiction. It is to acknowledge membership in an ecclesial institution which is anti-woman, while at the same time to affirm an inclusive, liberating insight of our time, namely, lesbian feminism. I appreciate the depth of this contradiction. I respect the choices that many women have made to drop the religious part of their inherited identity in order to make room for the full flowering of a lesbian feminist identity. However, I find that aspects of what it means to be Catholic, both historically and now, inhere in me in ways that will not go away, in ways that enhance my lesbian feminist being because of and not in spite of my Catholic up-bringing and how I perceive the tradition.

The central focus of this mini miracle is what I understand to be the justice-seeking aspect of Catholicism which has always been linked with efforts to love well. I wish to deepen this relationship, to claim it on its own terms, to wrest it away from the polluted parts of the tradition. This is not the work of apologetics but of reparations, a way of honoring the loving work of so many Catholic women over time. Further, I find that there are many female Catholics today whose justice-seeking work is the best of the tradition not of self-sacrifice but of self-fulfillment. While many do not call themselves lesbian feminists, I observe that they operate out of a very similar value system and, in many cases, out of a lifestyle which would be indistinguishable from my own. The reasons for their reticence in dealing with the lesbian aspect of who they are (they are often able to say feminist now, some years after the word has been demystified) are obvious in heterosexist patriarchy, and even painful when they are women in religious communities. But I trust that by showing how two fundamental parts of who I am are each challenged and enhanced by the attempt to hold them together I will lend clarity to others.

Catholicism, for my just pre and quite post Vatican II generation, has been a mixed blessing. On the one hand it is clearly aligned with the forces of social control which keep women, the poor (especially those in the two thirds of the world that does not control most of the wealth and power), and secular, nonclerical members of the church domesticated in a theo-political way. This is real and well known. It need not be elaborated except to be condemned. On the other hand, Catholic efforts to do justice have been exemplary and seductive in many instances. From my early teen years as a white, middle class, well educated Catholic (1964 and following, coinciding with the time of Vatican II), I have been involved in a range of social change efforts, most of which have had a religious referent. For example, I spent summers working with children in inner city neighborhoods or on Native American reservations; I did some social work in Appalachia; all of these efforts designed by well meaning church folks to put the boundless energy of the fortunate few to work for the needs of the unfortunate many.

I have since learned that such efforts were at best well intentioned yet totally misguided. Too many church-related justice efforts had too much proselytizing and too little emphasis on structural change with those in need leading their own campaigns for justice due and not charity given. But mistakes notwithstanding, the lasting impact on me was that there is no way to be Catholic without doing the concrete socio-political, justice-seeking work necessary to make any of the vision of the faith real. Not unrelated was the fact that co-workers in these efforts became my friends, my lovers, my *companeras* for the longterm commitment we knew it would take to make even the smallest changes. What was clear to us was that community would build among us, as it always had among women who have made common cause. Community comes from deepening goals into a consistent lifestyle of sharing. We found ourselves bonded as we tried to be consistent about our commitment and our lifestyle.

What was important then, and is even more so now in the Reagan years, is that government, big business and the university do not claim to seek justice. But the Christian community, in its many forms, does make such a claim. Because it makes this claim, and because it has a certain tradition and infrastructure for getting the work done, I see it as crucial from a faith posture, and from the point of view of effective political strategy, to use the base that exists. I also consider it important to hold religious people to their word, to invite a deeper coincidence between word and action. I admit that this dynamic of church concern was ingrained in me long before the development of a feminist consciousness, much less the dawning of a lesbian vision. But the impact has been to leave me with a sense that dogma, doctrine and liturgy are at best also-rans in a religious tradition which does justice. I had enough role models, enough fun and enough sense made of the Gospel claims to share resources that I could see then, and I affirm now, that justice work is the heart of Catholicism and that the pompous patriarchal rest is the tradition's tail. This is the insight which prompts me to work ecumenically and especially with those who profess no religious affiliation. Our unlikely coalitions for justice work.

Those youthful experiences which I have mentioned have given way to adult work with Catholic groups like NETWORK, New Ways Ministry, Women's Ordination Conference, Catholics for a Free Choice and Conference for Catholic Lesbians among others. These embody the religious values of old, but give them a powerful, empowering way of being useful for substantive structural change in church and society. My own work with WATER (Women's Alliance for Theology, Ethics and Ritual) is an ecumenical effort to facilitate feminist liberation theology, ethics and ritual for social change and community building. It is another example of how people and groups, many of whom have little if any relationship to the patriarchal institutional church, but claim continuity with the tradition of a "discipleship of equals" do the work of justice.[1] It is on this basis, claiming ourselves church, that we work, often overtime and for limited compensation, so that the unequal power equations that hold sway currently may be transformed.

This perspective is best expressed in the growing women church movement which collects the energies of many Catholic women's groups into a coalition for change. At a recent Witness for Justice sponsored by the Women Church Convergence the focus was clear:

> We stand here today as witness to the fact that the vitality that is Church is found in women-church....In women-church real justice is possible: the justice that comes of eyes that see, ears that hear, hands that touch and hearts that love the authentic experience of women....We call up the images of all our sisters who struggle for justice and who are the solution to whatever alienation and isolation the hierarchy experiences...[2]

The concrete works of justice, beginning as I have had to learn over the past fifteen years with justice for us as women, and not for everyone else first and only as if women were not oppressed, is what it means to express religious faith in a God/ess of love. It is what it means to be in continuity with generations of women and men who have found meaning and hope in the sharing of bread and wine as in the sharing of everything. While actively seeking to eradicate the patriarchal institutional Church, I am enthusiastic about embracing this brand of Catholicism. In so doing, with Elisabeth Schussler Fiorenza and others, I "claim the center" of the very tradition itself, and simply go about the work of justice.

My lesbian feminist formation has been equally compelling and probably just as long. From early on I realized that women love women, that women are marginalized and oppressed for a variety of class, race and ethnic reasons but also for being women. I knew that it was women who did the work and men who got the credit. I realized that it was women who kept the house, church or office in order and men who made the decisions. I knew that a dumb man was smarter than a brilliant woman, that an incompetent priest was better than a very able nun, that an irresponsible son was more desirable than a conscientious daughter. In short, I was taught that it is a white, wealthy man's world until women, people of color and the poor change it together.

Fortunately I grew up at a time when the organized women's movements would use the insights and struggles of women and men before us to turn the notion of equality into law and public policy, to change attitudes and accesses to power to reflect the values of inclusivity and mutuality which came to me, as to many others, via my religious tradition. For me to be a feminist, then, is to understand the historical and contemporary oppression of women on its own terms, and to see it played out with other forms of oppression, especially racial, ethnic and economic. To be a feminist is to be committed to a lifelong struggle to bring about the sharing of power and the equitable distribution of resources. To be a feminist is to pass on a more just world to the earth's children by taking women's oppression seriously. A feminist stance issues in action for change.

We have become reasonably astute about justice. We can see the lack of it and we know something about what might bring it about. But love is less obvious even in a religious tradition which claims it as its bottom line. Love, I have learned as a lesbian feminist, begins with loving oneself, something which women are systematically conditioned not to do in heterosexist patriarchy. To love myself as a woman is to defy the culture which, when bolstered by the Church, would have me fragment myself by insisting that self-love is solipsism rather than a springboard from which I can fully love others. Similarly, to love another woman in addition to myself in heterosexist patriarchy is to reject the social mores which dictate that women love men only, that women put men first, that women share intimately both psychically and physically only with men. To love women in a culture which forbids us to is to act justly. It is to put women first in a preferential option for those who have been left aside. It is to be open to and to cultivate friendships with women. Such friendships may, though do not necessarily, include sexual expression. But such friendships bear the full weight of women's love and celebrate its goodness, including women's right to genital expression with one another where appropriate.

What is significant is that this experience and insight about women's self and other love grounds our feminist insights and commitments in the embodiedness which heterosexist patriarchy fears most. The love we have for ourselves and for other women is expressed by concrete acts of care and support, in gesture and sharing. These "corporal works" of love are so varied: hugs, parties, long phone conversations, dancing, love making, sharing tea, mapping strategies, writing notes, creating rituals, protesting nuclear weapons, going to jail for opposition to apartheid, enjoying leisure. And they are what gives us the motivation and, at the same time, the strength to do the work of justice.

This love for women in our time is what it has always meant to be lesbian. It is to reject the culture's messages and to embrace our own best intuitions for surviving and flourishing in a society which would cut us off from ourselves and each other in a sinister yet effective effort to control us. This is what Adrienne Rich has called "the lesbian in each of us."[3] Claiming lesbian feminist identity and commitment and not simple feminist identity is a deliberate, intentional way of understanding and underscoring the embodied, sensuous part of who we are. It is to claim it for what it is, to take its energy for ourselves rather than to let it be defined for us. It is, finally, to fulfill the invitation to love the neighbor as the self without qualification.

Claiming to be lesbian feminist is to leave no question about the fact that embodied love and not abstract hate grounds our search for justice in a world and church which would have us deny ourselves. Claiming a lesbian feminist vision is to risk confusion and misunderstanding in order to get discussion going which will finally result in a triumph over heterosexism and homophobia. Claiming a lesbian feminist identity is an effort to love well, with all of its complications, to pave the way for friendships of every gender make-up which can reflect the values of inclusivity and mutuality.

Such friendships are nearly impossible in our society, made even more unlikely by the Church's baptism and confirmation of sexism and heterosexism. But I take it to be a social justice task of the first order to bring up children free from such biases, to make changes in laws and in insurance and employment policies which reflect the reality of same sex couples. I consider it a work of justice to instruct hospitals on new meanings of the term next-of-kin. These efforts are part of what it means to live "in right relation," just as we try to keep the U.S. from invading Nicaragua.[4] Our justice agenda is set by all acts which trivialize human lives, which lie about the reality behind the appearances.

This is why so many who say we are lesbian feminists are involved in a range of justice activities, because we see the connections between and among the many forms of oppression, beginning with how it affects our own lives. We have something to gain from every victory because it is linked with our own. We act, then, not out of pure altruism or pure self interest, but out of a deep insight into the interconnected web of oppression which must be undone for a beautiful network of liberation to unfold. It is slow work.

It is expected in my circles that to be a "politically correct" Catholic these days is to work against U.S. intervention anywhere, to lobby for increases in social services for the materially poor, to work for a woman's right to choose an abortion if her situation warrants. Of course I hold out the hope that my politically correct friends in those movements will figure out that their analyses and strategies must include educational and political efforts which will enhance a lesbian feminist vision of the Church and the society. Some groups have begun to do this work. Others are moving more slowly. But it is clear that the message is out and that justice groups cannot ignore it if they are to claim to function out of an inclusive vision of liberation. Of course I am not naive about the difficulty this presents, especially for gender mixed groups, but I am clear about how important it is, something which resistance helps me to measure.

The claims made by religious groups for liberation are useful for moving lesbian feminist insights from the closet to the mainstream. The universal search for justice, much touted by Catholics, must be based on the many particular forms of oppression. Theological leverage can be applied to show that groups have a selective, partial view if they fail to grapple with issues of embodied love. This is leverage one simply does not have with groups that operate from a single issue perspective or from a pragmatic base which includes no such lofty vision. Still, the fact that justice begins at home cannot be overstressed among those who have internalized the doing-for-others mentality rather than a mindset which stresses being for all of us. Such persons, in their frantic efforts to do justice, sometimes miss the need to love well. Burnout and bitterness often follow.

The consequences of bringing lesbian feminist insights to the justice community are serious. One can be dismissed easily, accused of mixing agenda, diverting from the real struggle.

Likewise, having anything to do with the Catholic Church (even explicit efforts to eradicate its patriarchal institution) are considered suspect among many lesbian feminists. In the social justice world, regardless of one's politically correct posture and work on other issues, this one takes the spotlight. Will I have credibility on the question of women's ordination if I articulate a lesbian feminist starting point and not simply a feminist one? Will I do more harm than good trying to prevent sexual harassment by clergy because I see things as a lesbian feminist? What will Latin American women think of North American lesbian feminists as we engage in common struggles? These inquietudes are played out in a range of ways from oppressively polite warnings to outright censorship. But more difficult is the extent to which silence sometimes reigns when people pass over the particularity of lesbian feminist struggles in favor of a homogenized view of oppression and liberation. This is very effective when the goal is to disempower, and would be considered intolerable if applied to any other issue. It is usually veiled heterosexism/homophobia but something that is being approached head-on as groups like the Conference for Catholic Lesbians gather strength. Then our sisters in the justice community will feel the need to look at the base of their own work, and see if it is indeed as empowering and liberating as it might be from a lesbian feminist perspective.

Ironically, there are many women in this kind of work whose relationships with women, whose way of sharing support and encouraging celebration are indistinguishable from my own. There are even cases of such women, including women religious and married women, whose primary relational commitments (including in some cases sexual expression) are with women. They tend to have a deep resistance to incorporating a lesbian self/community understanding for fear of how the word will label them in a hostile world. But I have confidence that in time their focus on justice will give way to a consideration of love. In heterosexist patriarchy there is simply no other way to name the reality of embodied love, nor is there, in my opinion, any more effective way of dismantling such structures than to use the term lesbian feminist as assurance that no part of it shall remain. The logic and the language follow the experience, but follow they do.

It is more difficult, frankly, to see how lesbian feminists will ever appreciate the value of a religious tradition as thoroughly patriarchal as Catholicism. I have tried to show that the institution can be separated (not completely, I admit, but enough to make it distinguishable) from the embodied imperative to do justice which has been received by many of us through the tradition. It is this active work that deserves respect, not the patriarchal packaging that many of us have long since left behind. Critiques of this will have an anti-Catholic ring, something which our Jewish sisters have taught us is intolerable when directed at one's religious heritage, whatever it may be. Curiously, much of what lesbian feminists want comes in this activist approach with religious background. The very work of love and justice is seen as the essence of the spiritual quest. The intersection of sexuality and spirituality is found here. Sexuality as embodied energy with an intentional focus is joined with spirituality as the ability to make choices while enhancing the quality of our lives together. Music, art, prayer, dance, meditation, healthy food, rituals of all sorts, express the integration of sexuality and spirituality.

We are renewed in a whole and holy way for the work of justice. We are grounded in communities of women friends who are unafraid of labels. When a lesbian feminist vision is connected to historical efforts to love well and to do justice, as in the Catholic case, horizons are expanded. Singer/songwriter Holly Near captures this insight:

> The world is full of lovers and friends
> Every town, city and land
> Gay people working for peace on this earth
> Courageous we take a stand.
>
> Good for the world for coming out...
> When we come out it's good for the world.

Long after lesbian/gay rights have been achieved in church and state, long after it becomes clear that a lesbian feminist analysis does not begin and end in bed, the questions will remain about those of us who have chosen and been chosen to bring these connections to consciousness. She could have had a brilliant academic career, if only she had not come out, some might say of me. Or, she would have been a great liturgist for the whole church if only her sexuality had not become an issue, might be said of a friend. Or, she could have gone sky high in the corporation if only she had not put her energies into CCL and had the wrong people find out about it, might be said of another. But the doubters miss the point. We have learned too well how change takes place, how people grow into new awareness, how connections between/among issues are made. We have been schooled in the necessity to make change, for justice's sake, because love demands it. This education has marked us forever; it is, some might say, the indelible mark and, try as we might, we cannot erase it. Nor do we want to in most cases, because this same effort to do justice beginning with our own lives has led us to other people, our friends, in some cases our lovers, in every case our companions in a fulfilling and integrity providing lifestyle that most of us would not trade.

We have been schooled in sacrifice but rejected it in favor of sharing. The model is one of abundance and not of scarcity. So I will teach outside of the university where most people are anyway, and my friend will do liturgies for Women Church and not in St. Peter's; the corporate friend will give valued business advice to all of us by whom she is deeply appreciated rather than being a functionary in a structure which does not care about her. This is neither sour grapes nor making a virtue of necessity. It is embracing the imperative to love well and to act justly; it is a matter of acknowledging what and who nourishes and compels us.

We have seen justice done before. We recognize it even in the seemingly unlikely places where so much more work is needed. Such an attitude articulated by Catholic lesbian feminists is the proof that there is a way to meld deeply rooted religious beliefs with the contemporary expectations of self- and community-conscious women. Women Church, CCL and justice-seeking women have much to gain by taking the combination seriously. We can teach each other as we go, lesbian feminists and Catholic justice-seekers, until one day we meet and realize that we have met before. May our numbers multiply.

1. Elisabeth Schüssler Fiorenza, *In Memory of Her*. New York: Crossroad, 1983. This is a central theme in Schussler Fiorenza's writings.

2. Statement of the Women Church Convergence at the "Witness for Justice," Washington, D.C. November 1985.

3. Adrienne Rich, "It is the Lesbian in Us..." New York: W.W. Norton and Co., 1979.

4. Carter Heyward, *The Redemption of God*. Washington, D.C.: University Press of America.

5. Holy Near, "Good for the World," words by Holly Near, music by Holly Near and Jeff Langley, recorded on the HARP album, Here for Music, Redwood Records, Oakland, California, 1984.

Blessed Are Lesbians Who Resist Their Oppressors, They Will Be Called Valiant Women

Resistance to oppression grows from the soil of lesbian awareness. Our love for women, our loyalty to our sisters is an act of defiance in a world which gives man first place. A tenacious faith in our own wisdom and experience steadies our conviction to speak with a lesbian voice. As we work to dismantle the power of oppressors, lesbian women are overturning the scriptural understanding of valiant women — from ideal wife to woman-loving resister.

Childhood Saints:
One - Maria Goretti

Martha Courtot

long after my childhood saints
have cracked, perished into dust
of cool reason
your small bony arms continue to clutch
  (the wounded body bleeds
   in some dark corner
   of my life)

we pretended you were a joke for us
they tried so hard to make you a saint
dragging your body up from the grave
hanging your withered arm
in a glass case
(the arm which resisted)
we carried your picture
in our purses
consigning ourselves secretly
to a future frigidity
fearful always of the knife
in the hands of the man
you lived with and trusted

there was some appetite loose in your house
it was sly and sickening
it walked like a man
you were supposed to trust him
but the day he found you alone
he moved his body against you
an accident which maims
his knife was secure in his lonely cool hand

you were supposed to trust him
your small body was vulnerable and pretty
everyone agrees
perhaps *you* were just growing
into some appetite you might one day
want to satisfy
but you held out against him

the Church told us it was your chastity
you protected with your life
but oh Maria, I can feel you
moving inside me
raising the withered resisting arm
your small warrior self
is not frightened of sexuality
but of violation

it was your self
whole intact
you refused to relinquish
to your attacker
not willing to give even one moment
of surrender
to this man
your body fell under his blows

your early death
flutters through my dreams
a bird wanting to escape
in and out of my choices
it flies
trapped in the deepest corridor
forgotten
locked away in some basement
of my mind
banging ruthlessly against dirty windows
no one can see through
it wants to fly free

i wanted to forget you
and your death

i lived
i lived and when the man came

the man with the knife
and sometimes he was a woman
i stepped forward
i lived and gave to him
those pieces of myself
he thought he wanted
i lived
opening the knife-soft places for him
just to make it easier
for him
to be more accessible
for him

i was supposed to trust him
i was supposed to trust her

and i lived

your resistance lived also
in me through me around me
your resistance grew in me
escape you whispered
escape the knife, you pleaded
escape or die

o this knife in the mind
o this knife in the heart
how it kills and goes on killing
forever
until that day i remember you
in my resistance
place my body against the enemy's will
refuse to surrender the light
at the center of my being

let them misunderstand you
Maria
the Church-Fathers
the men in our houses whom we trusted
the laughers and the sneerers
we who have been assaulted
and given in understand you

i name you for myself: saint

resistance fighter
even the Church cannot contain
your meaning

the twelve year old inside me
salutes you

and in the sweet open flesh love
river of appetite, passion, surrender in joy
i share with my lover
you have a part also
you showed me the way

now you come too

Entering into the Serpent*

Gloria Anzaldúa

"Sueño con serpientes, con serpientes de mar, concierto
malo y de serpientes sueño yo. Blancas, transparentes, en
sus barridas llevan lo que puedan arrebatar del amor. Oh,
oh, oh la mato y aparece una mayor."[1]

Silvio Rodriquez

No vayas al excusado en lo oscuro. Don't go to the outhouse
at night, Prieta, my mother would say. *No se te vaya a meter
algo por allá.* A snake will crawl in to your *nalgas,* make you
pregnant. They seek warmth in the cold. *Dicen que las culebras*
like to suck *chiches,* can draw milk out of you.

En el excusado in the halflight spiders hang like gliders. Under
my bare buttocks the deep yawing tugs at me. I can see my legs
fly up to my face as my body falls through the round hole into
the sheen of swarming maggots below.

Snakes, *víboras:* since that day I've sought and shunned them
Always when they cross my path fear, elation flood my body. I
know things older than Freud, older than gender. She — that's
how I think of la Víbora, female. Like the ancient Omecs, I
know Earth is a coiled serpent. Forty years it has taken me to
enter into the serpent, to assimilate the animal body or soul.

Ella Tiene Su Tono

Once we were chopping cotton in the fields of Jesús María
Ranch. All around us the woods. *Quelite* towered above me
choking the stubby cotton that had outlived the deer's teeth.

I swung the *azadón* hard. The *quelite* barely shook, showered
nettles on my arms and face. When I heard the rattle the world
froze.

I barely felt its fangs. Boot got all the *veneno.* My mother
came shrieking, swinging her hoe high, cutting the earth, the
writhing body.

I stood still, the sun beat down. Afterwards I smelled where fear had been: back of neck, under arms, between my legs; I felt its heat slide down my body. I swallowed the rock it had hardened into.

When Momma had gone down the row and was out of sight, I took out my pocketknife. I made an X over each prick, my body followed the blood, fell onto the soft ground. I put my mouth over the red and sucked and spit between the rows of cotton.

I picked up the pieces, placed them end on end. *Culebra de cascabel.* I counted the rattles: twelve. It would shed no more. I buried the pieces between the rows of cotton.

That night I watched the windowsill, watched the moon dry the blood on the tail, dreamed rattler fangs filled my mouth, scales covered my body. In the morning I saw through snake eyes, felt snake blood course through my body. The serpent, my *tono*, had given me supernatural power. I was immune to its venom. Forever immune.

Coatlalopeuh

The single most potent religious image of the Chicano-Mexicano is la Virgen de Guadalupe. She, like my race, is a synthesis of the old world and the new, the syncretism of the religion and the culture of the two peoples that make up the Chicano-Mexicano: the Spanish and the indio, the conquerers and the conquered. It is this middleground, this crossroad, that I, as a Chicana-Mexicana, growing up in the *frontera*, the Texas-Mexico border, am caught between. To me, la Virgen de Guadalupe is the symbol of ethnic identity and of the tolerance for ambiguity that Chicanos-Mexicanos, that people of mixed race, that people who cross cultures, by necessity possess. Today she unites people of different races, religions, languages. She mediates between the Spanish and the Indian cultures, or three cultures as in the case of Mexicanos of African or other ancestry, between the Chicano and the white world, and between humans and the divine — the world of spiritual entities. *Mi mamagrande Ramona toda su vida tuvo un altar pequeño en la esquina del comedor. Siempre tenía las velas prendidas. Ahí hacía promesas a la Virgen de Guadalupe.*[2]

Guadalupe appeared on December 9, 1531 on the spot where the Aztec goddess, Tonantsi ("Our Lady Mother" or "Our Sacred Mother"), had been worshipped by the Nahuas and where a temple to her had stood. Speaking Nahuatl she told Juan Diego, a poor Indian crossing Tepeyac Hill, that her name was María Coatlalopeuh, which means the "one who has dominion over serpents." Coatl is the Nahuatl word for serpent. Because Coatlalopeuh was homophonous to the Spanish Guadalupe, the Spanish identified her with the dark Virgin, Guadalupe, patroness of West Central Spain.[3]

From that meeting Juan Diego walked away with the image of la Virgen on his cape, Mexico ceased to belong to Spain, and la Virgen de Guadalupe began to eclipse all other male and female religious figures in Mexico and parts of the Southwest. Today, in Texas and Mexico, she is more venerated than Jesus or God the Father. To me and other Mexicanos, she is the symbol of the rebellion against the oppression by the rich and the upper and middle class and their subjugation of the poor and the indio.

The Spaniards and their Church desexed Guadalupe, took Coatlalopeuh out of her. Divided her. Thousands of years before the female Self and the female deities had been split into good and evil, white and black. With the Mexicanos this Self got split into la Virgen de Guadalupe-Virgen María and Tlazolteotl-Coatlicue and la Chingada; into virgin and puta, into Beauty and Beast.

Las invoco diosas mías, ustedes las indias sumergidas en mí que son mis sombras. Ustedes señoras que ahora, como yo, están en desgracia. Ustedes que persisten mudas en sus cuevas.[4]

Coatl

"Dead," the doctor by the operating table said. I passed between the two fangs, the flickering tongue. Having come through the mouth of the serpent, swallowed, I find myself suddenly in the dark, sliding down a smooth wet surface, down, down into an even darker darkness. Having crossed the portal, the raised hinged mouth, having entered the belly of the serpent, now there is no looking back, no going back. Why do I cast no shadow? Are there lights from all sides shining on me? Feet take me out of here. Ahead, ahead in the belly of the serpent, curled up inside its coils, the damp breath of death on my face. And I knew at that instant: if I didn't change I'd die. Then I heard thunder. It was my heart beating.

The serpent is the personification of the instinctual in its collective, impersonal, prehuman, and awesome aspects. It is the symbol of the dark sexual drive, the chthonic, the feminine which is related to the creative principle. The serpent, the most dreaded of all the animals: what better symbol for the body and everything that is loathsome and vile and rotting and decaying and growing old and getting hair and urinating and shitting than the serpent? Catholicism and most religions say that the body is dirty and vile and we should escape it because it is a prison. The flesh is a necessary evil, only the spirit is all important. Discard the body, let it rot.

I say everything is divine, including matter.

The snake, she was the original rebel. According to my interpretation of Christian mythology, if it hadn't been for her we never would have eaten of the fruit of the tree of knowledge of good and evil. We'd still be in paradise, that is, unconsciousness. *Eva, en el Jardín del Edén,* entered into the serpent, took a bite, and we all fell into consciousness, into the body, into sexuality. And what is sexuality if not knowledge of the body and its instinctual rhythms. The small bit of consciousness we humans increase each century, each millenia, is due to her. The serpent connects night and day, light and darkness, body and spirit, the earthly plane with the spiritual one.

Las Presencias

One of my chief gripes against institutional religions is their taboo against some kinds of inner knowledge. They fear the "unsavory" aspects of ourselves, what Jung calls the Shadow. But even more they fear the supra-human, the god in ourselves. Institutional religions fear trafficking with the spirit world. "The purpose of any established religion is to glorify, sanction and bless with a superpersonal meaning all personal and interpersonal activities. This occurs through the 'sacraments,' and indeed through most religious rites."[5] As far as I'm concerned, the Catholic Church fails to give meaning to my daily acts, to my encounters with the "other world."

Four years ago a red snake crossed my path as Ricardo and I walked back from the dining hall at the MacDowell Colony to our cabins. The direction of its movement, its pace, its colors, the mood of the trees and the wind and the snake — they all spoke to me, told me things. I, Gloria, a primitive, look for omens everywhere. Nothing happens by chance — not slipping on dog shit and hurting my knee. Everywhere I catch glimpses of patterns and cycles of my life. They say we're crazy Indians, deluded Mexicans.

We're not supposed to remember such events. We're supposed to ignore, forget, kill those fleeting images of the soul's presence, of the spirit's presence. We're not supposed to remember that every cell in our bodies, every muscle, every bone has the spirit in it, that the spirit isn't outside our bodies or above our heads, somewhere up in the sky with God. We, the dark-skinned, the queer, the persecuted, are showing up religion's errors and fixed conceptions about God and good and existence. Religious doctrines cannot survive our scrutiny. That's why we are a danger, why we're ostracized, why our native religions are called cults, our beliefs called mythologies. On the side of non-life, institutionalized religions impoverish all life, beauty, pleasure. They encourage fear and distrust of life and of the body; they encourage a split between the body and the spirit and totally ignore the soul; they encourage us to kill off parts of ourselves.

On the gulf where I was raised, *en el Valle del Río Grande* in South Texas, it was known among the Mexicanos that if you walked down the road late at night you would see a woman dressed in white floating about and, sometimes, peering out of the church window. She would follow those who had done something bad or who were afraid. Los Mexicanos called her la Jila. Some thought she was la Llorona. Then, I, an unbeliever, scoffed at these Mexican superstitions as I was taught to in school. Now, I wonder if this story and similar ones were ways used by the culture to "protect" members of the family, especially girls, from wandering. There's an ancient Indian tradition of burying the umbilical of an infant girl under the house so that she will never stray from it and her domestic role.

But, no matter to what use these spirits were put by the culture, it is evident to me now that the spirit world, whose existence the whites denied, did in fact exist. I have had many encounters with that world since then. Now I wonder if la Jila was the spirit of Tlazolteotl, Daughter of Night, traveling the dark terrains of the unknown searching for the lost parts of herself, or if she was la Llorona, whom many Chicanas claim is the spirit Ce Malinali, better known as la Chingada, looking for her lost children, los Chicanos-Mexicanos. I remember her following me once. She, a spirit-ancestor and other "presences," have followed me from apartment to apartment, city to city. I feel their presence in my room this very minute.

Los espiritus. Their exhalation blowing in through the slits in the door during those hot Texas afternoons, raising the linoleum under my feet. A wave of wind buffeting the house. Everything trembling.

* This is part of an essay which will appear in *Borderlands,* to be published by Spinsters/Aunt Lute Press in Spring, 1987. Translation of Spanish to English by Zulma Iguina.

1. From the song "Sueno con serpientes" by Silvio Rodriguez, from the album, *Dias y Flores* (Days and Flowers).
    "I dream of serpents, of sea serpents. I dream up an evil concert of serpents. White, transparent, in their sweepings they drag away what they can steal from love. Oh, oh, oh I kill it and a larger one appears."

2. Grandma Ramona always had a small altar in the diningroom corner. She always had candles lit. There she would make promises to the Virgin of Guadalupe.

3. Ena Campbell, "The Virgin of Guadalupe and the Female Self-Image: A Mexican Case History." In *Mother Worship: Themes and Variations* by James Preston, ed. Chapel Hill: University of North Carolina Press, 1982, p. 22.

4. I invoke you, my goddesses, you the indians submerged in me, who are my shadows. You, women that now, like me, are in disgrace. You who remain mute in your caves.

5. Olivia M. Espin, "Cultural and Historical Influences on Sexuality in Hispanic/Latin Women: Implications for Psychotherapy." In Carole S. Vance, ed. *Pleasure and Danger: Explorations in Female Sexuality.* Boston: Routledge & Kegan and Paul, 1984.

Saying Goodbye to Mary

Linda Marie

Before I went to a Catholic reform school I went to a Catholic day school. I was 11 years old and I fell in love with a nun. I spent day after day following my nun to morning Mass and Vespers, to Benediction (they did not have a private chapel in their convent). I sat in the rear of the church trying to decide which nun she was by studying the row of black veils in the front pew. I was going to grow up and be a nun of the same order, then I could kneel next to her. I imagined what these nuns did when they filed neatly out the door to their convent. I wondered if it was a sin to imagine we were all nuns together, smoking our cigarettes, lifting our skirts, showing off sexy garters, playing poker, then rushing to confession before teaching school in our neatly pressed habits.

I was a Catholic because my Southern Baptist mother married a Catholic and her family hated Catholics. Well, it seemed the thing to do. Her husband was a German and if he had lived in Germany during World War II, he would have made the perfect head of a concentration camp. His abusive behavior towards all of us (my mother and the kids) was subliminally accepted by the Church. The priest would look at his parishioners and know that twenty men in his parish were abusing their children and wives and not deal with it. As a consequence of my mother's husband's sexual abuse of me, I was sent to a Catholic reform school.

Working class was something the nuns taught us to strive for. "Marry a butcher or a truck driver or a store clerk and make a better life for yourselves." We stole each other's medals and holy cards and had fist fights in the chapel. And we all hated the girl chosen to crown Mary on her most holy day.

I learned it was totally uncool to express my love or regard for authority figures. Reform school is where I first learned I had a sexual choice — I could have sex with men, women or myself. It is very important to note that I would not have believed that I had a choice if I hadn't learned to reject adult authority figures.

I also learned in reform school how to smoke so no one knew you were smoking — and how to write. Not what to say, but how to sit in one place and put words on a piece of paper for hours on end. This was because the discipline was to sit facing a wall and write hundreds of times what we must not do. The only clever thing I came up with was how to write three lines at a time by holding three pencils tightly in my hand — a trick that required dexterity and sneakiness.

As Catholics, we were expected to tell every sin we committed. This could be any act we were for some reason ashamed of. These acts were categorized under such things as greed, lies and sex. I have not been to confession in over twenty years, yet I *still* carry a need to tell my secret acts to someone. I haven't done a single thing in my life that I could say, "No one in the whole world knows about that." I am quick to confess my latest sins to anyone who will listen.

Although I had problems identifying with God (man in beard who was ready to take people's lives and toss them to the fires of hell), I loved Mary. Mary was really the only being God would listen to because she was his mother. The priest who came to say Mass in the chapel at reform school would warn us to be sure to spend more time with God/Jesus than with his mother. We were made to feel guilty for spending too much time with Mary, who many of us substituted for real live mothers. After a while I became more and more aware of Mary's lack of breasts, hips, or body odor. She probably never had a period or picked her nose or even ate a hearty meal, let alone belched. For years I had a two-foot statue of Mary. I left her with my children and their father when I moved out.

Shortly after I moved in with my woman lover, I visited the kids. "I don't know how she lost her head," they tell me even now, six years later. Well, it was time, I think, to let it all go. What could be a clearer symbol than the mother of God having her head knocked off her sexless body?

Notes from a Catholic Daughter

Crystal Waverly

Girls are better than boys. Everybody in St. Cecilia's Grammar School knew that. The nuns thought so and what they thought was law — they were *always* right. Boys were noisy, sloppy, and constantly getting into trouble, as well as getting hit or having their knuckles smashed or ears pulled by some enterprising nun. Girls were obviously superior and since being perfect was what God wanted His children to be, boys were a step downward, closer to the everlasting fires of hell which awaited all those children who dared to ask too many questions, "doubt their faith," "think impure thoughts," or feel any feelings other than "holy feelings pleasing to God." To be human, i.e. natural, was an affront to the supernatural. The natural and supernatural were at war. In the characteristic catch-22 fashion of the Catholic Church of the 50's, by definition anything which emanated from us human beings was imperfect and was, therefore, displeasing or, at best, tolerated by the all-knowing, all-powerful, all-perfect Father who had favorites and would not hesitate to cast his enemies into "eternal damnation." Since we were born to "know, love and serve God," I was convinced that it was my own stubbornness and contrariness that prevented me from loving and adoring this image. Starting my life out relating to the highest power in the universe in a counterfeit and, at best, ambivalent manner felt uncomfortable and sneaky; although my true feelings remained under the surface they were not far enough under for me to feel guilt-free. Guilt became my daily companion, as much a part of my wardrobe as my coat. Taking off my coat, however, was easier than shedding the guilt. People were *supposed* to feel guilty. Hadn't Adam sinned so that now God despised us all and took pleasure in our discomfort over whether we were headed for heaven or hell?

Fortunately some of the more woman-hating aspects of the

Catholic religion were neutralized for me by this knowledge that boys were lesser beings than girls since boys were generally despised or dreaded by the nuns. The concept of Eve as the channel by which evil entered the human race did not get absorbed as deeply as it might have since everyone knew "boys were bad" and "girls were good." And since the Blessed Mother was the highest form of human being and never slept with a man, my preference for women seemed validated and perpetually reinforced. At that point in my life, I did not question the political ramifications of a male God; however, His arbitrary and vengeful way of dealing with His "creatures" solidifed my growing suspicion that males were defective in their lack of trustworthiness and compassion.

Why my anger was not directed more to the nuns is an interesting question. Perhaps I sympathized with their frustrated need for power, even if only over children. My strategy was to keep a low profile with God, i.e. minimal compliance, while getting lots of "protection" from the Blessed Virgin Mary. I felt safe with her and, since God liked her so much, anything she wanted, she could have. I trusted her. In a sense, she felt more powerful than God. He would never "cross her." And *she* didn't have to be with a man to please God. In fact, it pleased God if women stayed away from men. At least He and I agreed on that one. Did God hate himself? God even killed his own Son, yet he'd never lay a hand on Mary. She was the real Power. I knew I was safe with her and I knew she was *for* me, not against me. Liking girls was the only sensible thing to do. It might even keep me out of hell.

My first year in Catholic school, second grade, I was immediately drawn to the cutest girl in the class, Kathy. I was "smart" and she was "dumb," according to my mother. But cute is what I wanted and for some reason I was not shy about getting her as my best friend. We'd stand in the hallway during recess and touch tongues — probably when no one else was around, although I think people were around us sometimes. I felt on top of the world when we did this, powerful and in control, alive. However, second grade was when we had to make our first confession and so we learned about "sin" and "impure thoughts" and how to "examine our conscience." For a compulsive kid, this was a heavy trip. It taught me that I was bad. What would happen if I forgot something or held back a little in telling my "sins" to the priest, who took the place of God? I do not remember touching tongues after second grade — I wonder if that was related to learning about sin?

Second grade was tough. Sr. Meritas would step on my toes, but somehow I got the idea I was not supposed to say ouch. However, not saying ouch was viewed as being stubborn and not giving in. Her sadistic games made me feel that something was wrong with me — I was not lovable in her eyes nor God's. Since my writing looked like "chicken scratch" to her, I was deserving of divine retribution, or at least rejection. Being better than the boys was only a small consolation — at heart I thought I was rotten, deserving of God's most fearful punishment because this nun could not love me. I was guilty for being alive; what right did I have to experience joy? God would really get me then. At least if I was guilty, it would look like I was trying to be good. At heart I felt I could never be good enough to please God, whom I feared and distrusted.

After a while, I didn't even want to please God but we all know what happened when Lucifer rebelled against Him. God didn't like dissenters or people who thought their own thoughts. Actually, there were no "own thoughts." There were either God's ways or the devil's ways. Any thoughts or feelings contrary to God's ways were planted in us by the devil because the human heart was "wicked" and in rebellion toward God. We humans were "fallen creatures" and deserved to be abused — by the nuns and God. The fact that they were abusive seemed to prove that we were bad. And to make absolutely sure that we rejected and despised ourselves we were taught that self-denial was the most pleasing thing to God. If we, too, rejected, denied, and despised this "self" which was "at war" with God, then God would love us and we would "be saved" from ourselves and the devil. It's amazing we didn't become schizophrenics. If we dared love this "self" which was evil, we'd be damned. The price of heaven was self-hatred. We could not save ourselves — we were too wicked; God had to save us from His wrath.

God was jealous, too. If we loved ourselves more than we loved Him, we were in serious trouble. And all power came from Him so that all homage was due to Him alone. Any other powers, spirits, or even names for God were forbidden. Other religions were "in error." We had "the truth." And if we were foolish enough to question or doubt it, hell would be worse for us, because God had given us the truth and we rejected it. "Woe to you..." intoned the nuns, as well as the priests from the altar. God wanted us to suffer. It made us pleasing to Him. God seemed to me to be a sadistic monster whom we *should* love. There was no escape — we had heard "the truth." It was harder for Catholics to get to heaven, but you couldn't not be Catholic once you were one. No exit.

Third and fourth grades droned by with the same messages burned into our brain cells on a minute-to-minute basis. I still thought Kathy was the cutest girl around and one day I got lucky as she agreed to spend the afternoon at my house. For whatever reason, we ended up taking a bath together and I remember initiating a game of wrapping ourselves in towels and then letting the towels come undone so we could peak at each other naked. Somehow, sex and "impure thoughts" were not applied to girls; no one even acknowledged the existence of lesbians or gay men; and, since girls were more pleasing creatures to God, loving them felt okay (although I instinctively knew I should not *talk about* loving them).

When I was 10, I went to a summer day camp and immediately fell in love with Cynthia. She was cool. We'd walk hand in hand all over the camp and one day I asked her to go steady. Somehow I knew girls were supposed to go steady with boys, but I hoped she didn't know that yet. We went steady that summer and I felt so lucky and secure. It never occurred to me to be sexual with Cynthia; I just knew I loved her and wanted to be with her.

Sixth grade was a strange year. I was the nun's definite favorite. I couldn't tell if she had a crush on me or if she favored me because my mother sewed for her. Whatever the reason, I felt something was "strange" about her feeling for me. There were also vague rumors about her heavy friendship with a female nurse. I started to get the impression that some relationships were "sick" and that it had to do with being close. These very diffuse feelings made me ripe for a case of homophobia. When Sister Gertrude left the convent the following year, my feelings were confirmed. Something was "wrong" with her friendship with Agnes, the nurse. Was I tainted too because Sr. Gertrude loved me? I was already learning to discount the truth of my own feelings, my joy at being with girls, and to accept the vague, but definite message that women who loved each other "too much" were "unhealthy." Or maybe Sr. Gertrude and Agnes felt sick about their relationship because they heard the same message. I'll never know. There was no place to turn; the poison of homophobia, as yet unnamed, was like the air — it was everywhere; it existed just as if it were reality itself.

My own feelings at this point were directed toward idolizing Elizabeth Taylor, the movie star. I remember the power, joy and strength of those feelings, and my mother's words, "You'll grow out of it some day," with the implicit message that somehow this was not right. Quietly I resolved that I would not give up this joy, that it was real, not transitory.

Sixth grade was also when I had a crush on a boy. I used to fantasize kissing him. My guilt knew no bounds over these "evil desires" and I became depressed and listless. Finally, in order to regain my energy, I had to "confess" to my parents that I had been desirous. From the trauma of experiencing normal feelings, I can only infer how deeply ingrained was the split between permission to have human feelings and being acceptable to God and parents. Viewing God as Super-Parent meant that becoming responsible and self-directed were sins that would lead me astray. I would become overly willful. Spiritual infantilism appeared to be a virtue rather than the crutch and defense that it is.

The seventh grade nun did me in. She was demoted from teaching high school and bitterly resented being with us. Her excessive demands, including homework until midnight each night, played on my perfectionist nature until I was strung tighter than a violin. In self-defense I left St. Cecilia's Grammar School and entered the cold, impersonal world of a public junior high school. I felt cast out from the womb, ejected from the Garden of Eden (hellish though it was), and somewhat confused by the dawning awareness that I might never love a boy. Another double bind: I seemed to fear not loving boys as much as I feared loving them.

The attention of the junior high boys made me uncomfortable as I began to realize my feelings were not what people wanted me to feel. Time to hide again, just as in second grade when I had to hide my rebellious feelings toward God. Layer upon layer of camouflage. I felt like a stranger on this planet, as if I had to go through life in disguise. I hadn't yet realized that only I could give myself permission to be, that my authorities, the Church especially, would never grant me that freedom. Five short years of Catholic schooling carved themselves so deeply into my mind and heart that, a quarter-century later, I am still dealing with the after-burn.

All names and places in this essay have been changed to protect the privacy of individuals mentioned.

Defect of Consent

Jennifer DiCarlo

"My wife was incapable on physiological-psychological grounds of consummating the marital act, the very attempt at it always evoking intense pain."

These words were written by my former husband in his petition for annulment presented to the Marriage Tribunal. He probably wrote them in answer to the questions in the guidelines: "Was the marriage consummated? If not, why not?" In the printed guidelines for my response I was asked similar questions. I chose, however, not to answer them.

Before formulating the petition, my former husband had consulted a professor of canon law who had informed him that "vaginism" falls under canon 1084§1 of the Code of Canon Law. Vaginism occurs when the vagina constricts so as not to allow the penis to enter. The canon lawyer had explained to him that vaginism can be of psychic or physical origin. As I sit writing this, I turn to one of the commentaries on canon law which I purchased in order to prepare myself for the annulment process. Under 1084§1 "Impotence," it says that frigidity does not constitute grounds for impotence. The issue is not one of pleasure but rather whether the wife possesses a vagina capable of receiving a penis. According to canon law such a vagina is necessary for procreation, one of the principal purposes of Catholic marriage.

The Marriage Tribunal did not grant an annulment on the grounds of canon 1084. My not responding to this point was, presumably, one reason. I know that I could have helped my former husband by supplying the Marriage Tribunal with information on my vagina. I could have confirmed his statement by describing the constant state of cramp in my vagina. I could have gone to a physician, psychiatrist or psychologist to obtain further testimony. Probably I would have had to allow myself to be examined by these professionals, to describe my vulnerability to them, to request that they bring expert testimony to the Tribunal of the truth of my words. I could have gone a step further and reported that I am an incest survivor. I could have described how when I was a pre-school child my vagina was ripped open by my father's penis penetrating me. Would that have made a difference to the Tribunal? I do not know.

The reason I do not know is that I feel that their questions, and in fact the whole process, were like my father's penis: aimed to penetrate me against my will. Oh, the Advocate of the Tribunal assured me that I did not have to answer any questions I did not wish to answer. If I did not cooperate, of course, my former husband's chances of obtaining the annulment would be lessened. For him, the annulment is of professional consequence. I thus knew that my not answering questions put to me by the Tribunal could mean significant disadvantages for my former husband.

Concern for his professional future led my former husband to petition my present archdiocese for the annulment, rather than submit it to the Marriage Tribunal of the diocese in which we both resided at the time of the separation and divorce. Neither he nor I believe that secrecy is strictly maintained; that is, we both assume that the upper echelons of the church hierarchy could gain access to information concerning an annulment. My former husband felt that his report concerning my sexuality could reflect poorly on him and hurt his professional advancement.

Vaginism was not the issue to which he devoted the greatest attention in his petition, but instead my being a lesbian. He deliberated on this issue at great length and in some detail. He emphasized that he had done everything possible to reach a reconciliation, even offering to continue the marriage if I would only give up my lesbian inclinations. In canon law terms, being a lesbian constitutes a "psychological incapacity."

I could have responded here also by confirming that I am a lesbian. I chose not to. My former husband was furious with me, calling my behavior "shameful." He reported that his family and friends were also deeply disappointed in me. I was the only witness who could reveal the "true reason" for the failure of our marriage. Why did I choose not to confirm that I am lesbian? I did want him to obtain the annulment. I certainly did not want him bound eternally to me — unable to remarry within the Church, and suffering professional losses. We had previously agreed that I would speak about my lesbian existence in my response. However, the situation had now changed. My former husband had made my lesbian existence known to my boss, a close friend of his, at the time of our separation. This action led to significant professional difficulties for me. With his petition he was informing church officials of the archdiocese in which I presently work of the same fact that had led to severe repressive measures at my previous place of work.

Will my name be placed on a list? Will a note be added to my file? As I write, church officials in New York City are actively campaigning against legislation protecting lesbians and gay men from discrimination in housing, employment and public accommodations. Why should church officials maintain discretion among themselves about lesbian and gay Catholics? Perhaps my former husband's claim, even if left unconfirmed by me, can lead to disadvantages for me in the future.

The image of the all-male Tribunal reading details of my intimate life made me ill. The possibility of my having to testify in person threatened a further invasion of my person. Again, I was not forced, only told that this was a borderline case and that I could help the case by coming for an interview. I was told that the interview was informal, alone with one man, and would be taped. When I inquired which questions would be asked, the advocate simply repeated the areas outlined on the written form. I asked him if he had read the cover letter accompanying my response, in which I had described several of the questions as inappropriate intrusions into the private sphere and had noted how especially problematic it is for an all-male Tribunal to be posing such questions. He responded with, "Oh, about the all-male Tribunal. Yes, we're aware of that." I said I would be informing him about whether I would come or not. I thought about it and discussed it with friends, and I made the choice not to go.

Yet, in spite of all this, the Marriage Tribunal granted an annulment. The grounds were "defect of consent," that is, "the respondent's defect of consent by reason of her absence of marital intention." Given the choice between describing to the Tribunal intimate details of my sexuality and describing myself as rebellious, as not consenting to Catholic teaching, I chose the latter path. I did what I could to describe myself essentially as a bad Catholic. I underscored that I did not believe in the indissolubility of marriage. I stressed that I did not want to have children. I pointed out that at the time of the marriage I had been hesitant as to whether within the institution of marriage the full equality of women and men could be realized. I said that it was clear to me that if my marriage were not such an institution I could not remain within it, and that I had discovered, in fact, that it was not such an institution. I consciously put myself at odds with the official Catholic teaching on marriage. My former husband in his testimony emphasized my involvement in the women's movement and the connection between my being a feminist and being a lesbian. He stressed that he accepted the official church position concerning marriage, not going out of his way to say that he too does not believe in the indissolubility of marriage.

The route of defect of consent seemed to me the only route that I could take with any integrity. I rebelled against the official church teaching intellectually and stressed that my intellectual commitment was related to my praxis, while refusing any details of my personal life. By doing this I made myself vulnerable to charges of running counter to official church teaching, but this seemed to me less of an intrusion into my own person.

I felt the irony and appropriateness of the Tribunal's decision when I received the letter granting the annulment for defect of consent. I do have a defect of consent. I do not consent to the Catholic understanding of marriage. I do not consent to being married. I do not consent to the intrusion of the Tribunal into my life. Perhaps my rejection of the attempts to interview me, to learn, "Was the marriage consummated? If not, why not?" and my not responding to the details given by my former husband were actions that symbolized to the Tribunal my defect of consent.

I now see that I have come full circle because of these experiences. In recent days I have begun to remember more of my incest experiences as a child. I remember with great pain and I know that there is enormous pain to come as I am able to remember more. I also now remember that the Catholic Church seemed to me a safe place, safe from the sexual advances of my father, a safe alternative haven. The incest occurred from when I was approximately three until I was approximately seven: at that time my father, who was an atheist, died. Towards the end of his life he began taking religious instruction and, in fact, was baptized on his deathbed.

When I was raped at age fifteen, I asked the rapist about his religious belief. I did not understand at the time why I was doing that, but I think I now understand it. I asked him, "Are you an atheist?" I had not made the connection with my childhood experience until a few days ago. I think that what I meant by the question was: you must be an atheist if you would do such a thing to a woman or young girl. My father was an atheist. Are you an atheist? You are doing what he did. The rapist said that he was an atheist and wondered why I asked. I think I felt that a person who believed in God might treat a woman or a young girl differently. That is what I had been led to believe as a child. The belief that men who believe in God will treat women and girls with some respect probably contributed to my intense religious involvement as a child.

I remember as a child the quiet and peace of the church. I would often go for visits to church during the school lunch hour. The church's peacefulness and beauty were very important to me. I remember my first communion, the parochial school, the nuns, the school uniforms; the environment felt protective. My father was no longer alive and the horror of my pre-school experience was over. It seemed that the trauma had passed and that here was a safe place, a place where there would not be an intrusion into my body. I think that the ideal of chastity played a role here, that is, being taught by women whose bodies were not intruded into by men. Being part of an atmosphere in which overt sexual expression was not encouraged had a calming and reassuring effect on me. Here was a place to develop intellectually, a place to ask questions, a place where I would not have the horrors that I had experienced. I also recall priests who had sexual interest in me. For example, when I was raped at the age of fifteen, my mother wanted me to speak with the priest. When I spoke with him — I did not see the necessity of it, but I did go to him because my mother had told me that I should — I think it was probably titillating for him. He told me the story of a woman who had been raped and who had nevertheless not had an abortion. She had rather given birth to the child and loved the child. I think this was the lesson he wanted to teach me.

So it was that from an early age I had a uniform impression of the Catholic Church as a place of safety, but my earliest experiences with the Church were not shaped by priests but by the nuns in my daily world of parochial school. Those experiences set me on a journey that has just now come to an end, that is, a journey of searching for safety, a haven where I could grow, think and develop. The experience with the Tribunal concerning the annulment has shown me that the Catholic Church is not that place, that, in fact, the intrusion of my father, who was an atheist, is in a continuum with the intrusion of the Tribunal which claimed not to be atheist. I see that this intrusion is not an accidental intrusion, but rather is meant to teach women to be heterosexual, in fact to train women to be victims. I have the image before me of what is required for a marriage according to canon law, of what consent implies. I have the image of the vagina waiting to receive the penis. The vagina which closes, which is defective in its consent, invalidates the marriage.

I do not identify myself as a lesbian in negative terms, as one who rebels against marriage. Instead I have described experiences with those who tried to make me heterosexual, and told how I have now received a document, signed and sealed, testifying to my defect of consent. But this defect of consent by reason of absence of marital intention does not confirm my lesbian existence, and it would require another essay to describe the strength that I have from being lesbian. That strength does not fit into the world of canon law, of incest, of rape. I think I have made a step forward by being able to identify and define myself in such a way that my defect of consent has become clear. The strength of being a lesbian, the strength of loving another woman, the strength of not being a victim is not accessible to canon law, nor to the theology that lies behind canon law, nor to the ideology that made it possible for my father to cause me so much pain and damage. The only thing that is visible is the defect of consent, that is, it is only at the point of intersection with those trying to penetrate me that my strength becomes evident to them, and the only way it can be seen and categorized is as a defect of consent. The woman should consent to being penetrated. The woman should consent to be impregnated. The woman should consent to taking on child care responsibilities. The rebellion against male dominance has to be phrased negatively. It cannot be phrased in active opposition, but has to be phrased as a *defect* of consent. The consent which is supposed to be present is not present. Consent is the norm and this is deviation from the norm.

In the years to come I will be thinking about the implications of what has happened to me and of how I have responded; I am learning to respond in ways other than the ways I responded as a child to my father's penetration. Defect of consent is not the origin of my spirituality. Rather, the strength that I discover in myself, the power that works alone in me and that I think can work within a relationship with another woman is the origin of my spiritual life. I want to think more about that in the coming years.

Message from Argentina*

Fulana de Tal

Dear Barbara:

Latin American countries do not have stability. I imagine that the United States government has a lot to do in the matter. Therefore, your letter arrived a month later because since Christmas we have had a mail strike which ended only a few days ago.

The topic that you propose is of interest to me. I appreciate your letter but, due to the rigidity of the Catholic Church and of our traditions that emanate from such a church, we do not have the right to say publicly that we choose to be lesbian. For this reason I would not want my name to be public. Although I have freedom to expose liberation theology, feminism, and the theories of Paulo Friere, if my name came out in a publication making a declaration about lesbian relationships they would possibly expel me from my position. Only recently have we allowed ourselves to say that we accept bisexuality as natural.

One of the elements that I rescue from my Catholic formation referring to lesbianism is that physical intimacy outside of sacramental marriage is a mortal sin. Therefore to have a sexual relationship that was not within Holy Matrimony and with the purpose of having children did not enter my head. Sexual pleasure was not a topic I could discuss with anyone in my adolescence. I felt attracted to women and men since my adolescence, but never went further than to hold hands or to dare a furtive kiss. I never thought that it was worse to be in love with a woman; I simply knew that I could not marry her, and that invalidated any future plans. When I was fifteen years old, my mother read a letter to a girl I was in love with. I did not say in the letter that I loved her, but the tone of the letter was affectionate. My mother told me that these demonstrations of love were very dangerous — without giving me details.

When I was twenty and studied theology, the professor of morals, a priest, never touched the subject of sexual relationships. In the books we were required to study, all material related to homosexual relationships or bestialities (sex with animals) was in Latin — a subject we did not study.

I was a nun for six years (I came out at twenty-nine). While I was in the convent I began to feel attraction for other nuns and students. This occurred at an institute for women who were taking university level courses. Nothing materialized due to the chastity vow, but many nuns were in love with each other.

After coming out of the convent I began to have lesbian relationships, but physical intimacy was always a mortal sin. The confessor's comments were always ridiculous. It was a "sickness," a "deviation," or "something unnatural." My study of social sciences helped me to accept cultural relativism, to overcome feelings of fault and sin, and to understand that what we do in love has a value in itself. Feminism in the seventies helped me to discover freedom of choice and I accepted lesbianism as something totally natural, but I don't think I have been able to erase the wounds of so many years of Catholic formation related to the sixth commandment. When my lesbian relationships become sexual, something changes in the friendship. There is a desire for possession, jealousy and frustrations that break the good friendship that existed. All of this could have something to do with the patriarchal structure of the Catholic Church. Friendship makes us equal, but the sexual relation becomes impregnated with clerical "machismo" (from other religions as well) that destroys equality and changes it into inequality — a distortion coming from the only one (according to patriarchal law) "normal" relationship between human beings, which is the heterosexual one.

In today's Argentina, lesbianism is not accepted although in feminist circles the topic is treated with a certain freedom. All the lesbians in the country know each other, or at least we know of others in different provinces. In the Federal District there is more freedom due to the anonymity of large cities, but in the provinces lesbianism is looked upon as a disgrace and it is very difficult to live it normally. There is a group of gay men in the Federal District who come out into the streets in homosexual demonstrations, but you never see women. It seems to me that males in general (gay or not) accept gay relationships with more ease because men are free to have sexual relationships with whomever they wish during their lives. It is true that a man who chooses gay relationships is not well accepted, but people do condone it, because his sexual needs are normal for him. On the other hand, in regard to women, any sexual relationship outside of marriage is not well accepted. Lesbianism would be a total liberation from male dependency and they are not going to allow it so easily. For now, it is something prohibited in public. We remain hidden.

> With love and a great hug,
> Fulana de Tal

*Translation by Maria Formoso

Blessed Are Lesbians Who Live Their Own Truths, They Will Grow in Wisdom

Lesbian existence is an invitation to immerse ourselves in woman-centered reality and to deepen our understanding of the significance of loving women. We walk the lesbian path with self-affirming faith, sensitive to the particular truths that flow from lesbian love. What we learn on our journey is that our wisdom and joy are commensurate with our being all of who we are.

You Remember Sophia

Valerie Miner

"Despina, you remember Despina," instructs the ancient woman as she sits on the stone steps frying sardines. "Despina has four children. You remember Despina."

"*Nai*," nods Sophia in the Greek which comes easily to her head but slowly to her lips. Speaking the old language is like trying to communicate through Novocaine. Numbness. She feels such numbness. Her eyes are drawn down to the sea.

"And Eleni. She lives in that big stone house by the *kastro*. Her husband is a farmer and she has five boys."

"*Nai*," nods Sophia, searching for her mother in this bird wearing thin, black cotton. Her face is struck as coldly as those clay tourist medallions and her silver hair, knotted at the back, is like a miser's purse, deceptively small.

"Yes, Mama, I remember," she wants to say. "And Sophia has no children. But she has a life. Born of farmers on the Island of Lesbos, she is now a doctor in a big American city hospital. She lives with the woman she loves. But Mama, you are too busy seeing what I am not."

Sophia knew it would be like this. Gone twenty years and still she knew. Knew in that part of herself which was deeper than memory. Which would sprout red poppies and pink daphne in dark dreams. She is dark enough to be taken for Chicana by the Americans. And Western enough to be taken for American by the shopkeepers here. Until they looked closely enough, to see she is one of their own, a Greek woman returned to Lesbos.

"You are happy?" Mama considers this prodigal daughter in the crimson trousers and the boy-short hair. She looks into reflections of her own amber eyes and asks, "You are happy, my little one?"

Sophia, the red giant, finds a tear on the edge of her smile. "*Nai*," she feels the numbness wearing down.

After dinner, Sophia says she will visit the sea. Avoiding her mother's hurt, confused glance, she walks quickly from the house. Mama cannot object. Their reunion is too fragile for demands. Questions cause enough strain.

Boys shout in the street. At first, Sophia is charmed by the chords of children's voices, a noise she never hears above the Los Angeles traffic. She is touched by the natural sound. And then she recalls her own childhood inside — practicing quiet over the washing. Murmuring. Always murmuring, even the prayers. Now all around her, she can see boys. Replicas of her old friends Christophe, Stevenos and Darius. Boys' voices. She cannot hear the silent, indoor girls. Perhaps, she laughs to herself, they have all gone to the sea.

Sophia can hear it still, the chorus of thirty years before. "To go to school for a girl is luxury." "Your parents are peasants, not nobility." "The money belongs in your dowry." "Six grades is enough." "Why must you go to Petra, all the way to Petra for school?" "It will turn your head." "It will..." And they were right. Ever since Petra, Molivos was too small for her long legs and big feet. It was in Petra that she met Stellio who promised an automobile and a big house like in the movies, if she would move with him to Los Angeles. After all, Los Angeles was where they made the movies. That she knew, even before Petra.

Walking down through the market now, all she can hear is the simmering of large black flies and fecund bees in the wisteria. The *tavernas* are quiet. Men are still at home eating meals their wives have spent all day preparing. As she passes the shop called "Agora," Sophia sees her hills have turned a California gold. Haze in the background. (And beyond that, Turkey. Turkey is just eight miles away. Eight miles to the enemy. Eight miles of brilliant blue between Europe and Asia.) Reminding her of Los Angeles. Reminding her that it was never like the movies.

The rape scene was the only place Stellio resembled Clark Gable and he was disappointed she wasn't as grateful as Vivian Leigh. Their marriage lasted one year. But it wasn't a complete loss. It lasted long enough for her to learn about community colleges, to meet a few women friends.

Hard to write Mama about the divorce. Hard to read back her shame, her bitter, "I told you so." How, then, could she write about going to college, about loving Myrna, about her dreams of becoming a doctor. Instead she wrote that she was well, working hard. She said she missed the bird music of Molivos. Mama asked the priest to read and write the letters. (She could have asked the teacher or one of the shopkeepers, Sophia knew, but she chose the priest.) Through Father's tense, spider scrawl, Mama wrote again and again, "I pray for your safe return."

Two American women at Stratos' *taverna* stare and smile. American. They have to be American with that size and bearing. Which she herself now shares. Almost. Their smiles blur into uncertainty as they regard each other, wondering if she is, after all, one of them. Sophia understands. She smiles hello. But she cannot reassure them. She does not know if she is American. Another time she might stop to talk ambiguities. Another time she might explain the banking hours and the best shops for jewelry and the status of Greek women. But now she must reach the sea.

Gulls sail low, scouting the last catch. The sky is washed a pale dark which Sophia remembers preceded the false promise of sunset. Donkey shit on the cobblestones. How could she explain to Myrna that she missed this smell? Overripe plums are splattered on the roadside. Such richness. *Star Trek* blares in Greek from an open doorway. The sea looks rougher than a moment ago, more determined, as if calling for the sun to set, summoning the moon to rise.

"A doctor now," Mama wrote, the priest wrote, both comprehending nothing except new access to her. "So now you can return home and do good." How could she explain her choice to work with immigrant families in America — mostly Mexican or Asian — rather than with her own people? If you were a person, who were your own people? If you were a gull, you were not a dove. If you were Greek, could you be an American? Was this the same water which washed through people in Tokyo and Santiago and Vancouver?

These beach rocks hold her steadier than city pavement. Lapping waves soothe her deeper than Stratos' *metaxa*. Shadowed hills, now almost invisible, call her to join the sleeping shapes in the distance. The hills. The sea. She had always been torn, even as a child.

Despina has four children.

Eleni lives in a stone house.

Mr. Spock speaks Greek.

The priest admonishes.

American women nod in tentative complicity.

She knew it would be like this. Twenty years away and she knew she would be drugged by the flowers. She knew Mama would hold her at arms' length like a stranger, her eyes still filled with longing for the daughter to return. Sophia knew she would return to the sea.

Here in the moonrise, she sees a face. Just beyond the cove, Sophia sees a moon face shining in the Aegean. Should she slip these fine lavender rocks into her red pants and wade out to this face?

Sophia does not have four children.

Sophia does not live in a stone house.

Closer still, she finds a seductive smile, which does not question, which does not blur, a clear face beaming from the sea, a reflection not of the moon, but of Sophia.

Sophia has a face which shines in the sea. It has always been there. Waiting for her. Ever since she was "odd Sophia with the books." Now she has found it again.

She stands in darkness an hour, beckoned by this luminous face in the sea. Her own moon floating within reach.

Sophia, you remember Sophia. Finally, the face finds a voice. She watches for another hour and decides she does not need to go as far as the cove. She does not need to explain herself to the Americans at the taverna or to the priest. She will rest easily at Mama's tonight. She will return to Myrna in Los Angeles. She salutes her reflection and turns back to Molivos.

The face she carries with her, between the lands, behind the shadows, beneath the waters. Sophia, you remember Sophia.

Less Catholic than the Pope

Margaret Cruikshank

When I think of myself as a Catholic schoolchild, I vividly recall humiliation at the hands of an old Irish priest who was pastor of the Cathedral parish and an occasional visitor to my third grade class. One day, his fat stomach pressed against the nun's desk in the front of the room, he asks, "Do any of you think you are good children?" As I raise my hand I see that nobody else has taken the risk — do they smell a rat? Father Corbett thunders his denunciation. How dare I presume to call myself a good child? Had I ever committed even the slightest venial sin? Of course I had. We are all sinners in the eyes of God. None of us can claim to be good. He ridicules me for my presumption.

I was mortified but only because I had miscalculated. I knew I was a good child, by my own reasonable standard. Who could live up to impossibly rigid standards? This insight did not free me from domination by the Church but my stubborn interior response to Corbett's blast at least allowed me to have my own point of view, in opposition to the official one.

Scene two, from my early twenties. A grad student at Loyola, I'm in the confessional at Holy Name Cathedral in Chicago. I confess to masturbating. The priest yells, "Get a boyfriend." I am humiliated. But knowing his advice to be truly dumb, even though I don't yet know I'm a lesbian, I decide to stop going to confession. I don't remember that I worried about becoming "habituated to sin." Probably the concept of mortal sin was dying out in me. Again, I spoke to no one about my feelings and when I stopped going to Mass a year later I didn't even speak to myself about separation from Rome. This was in 1965, when the campus chaplain's pro-war sermons made Mass intolerable. I decided that any church worth belonging to would be leading an anti-war movement. Now that view seems naive but at the time it was liberating. Later I did go to Mass occasionally with my first lover, but my faith must have been very relaxed because letting myself act on long suppressed lesbian feelings didn't cause me any religious doubts or guilt. Given the fervor of my youth and adolescence, this escape is rather surprising. It's as if the harsh, puritanical parts of Catholicism slipped off of me, perhaps because the pleasures of being sexual were strong enough that no rules could have held me back. So, instead of "falling away" (a phrase that makes me think of a cliff suffering from erosion), I experienced the Church falling away from me.

For the past twenty years, my attitude towards the works and pomps of Catholicism has been one of indifference, or at least that has been my idea of the proper attitude. Anger I tried to avoid because I saw that angry ex-Catholics were still very much caught up in Rome. If I ever glanced at a *Commonweal* or *America* (read so zealously when I was young), they seemed so narrow I couldn't read them. On the other hand, I still *felt* very Catholic. Any news about the Church in the media I paid close attention to, bits of information about what was going on interested me, and I could gossip for hours about Church personalities. When the encyclical on the pill came out, I was sorry that the Pope had blown it.

When I got a post-doctoral fellowship at the Benedictine Abbey and university in Minnesota, I felt a bit of a fake because I considered myself an atheist. As it turned out, I entered wholeheartedly into the ecumenical life of the fellows and when my turn came to plan a liturgy I did it enthusiastically. I went to the monks' prayers, chanted and sung, and found them uplifting. I suppose the emotional satisfaction of worship was strong enough to allow me easily to overlook the content. I probably would have felt some rebirth of interest in Catholicism as a personal choice (as opposed to a cultural inheritance) except for one huge drawback: the sexism I was beginning to be aware of in 1973 and 1974. One night the male fellows were invited to eat in the monks' refectory. I was excluded of course. I was not enough of a feminist then to find this outrageous. I thought it was amusing, especially since I vaguely remembered a rule that if a woman enters the monastery it must be reconsecrated. This knowledge gave me an eerie sense of being passive and powerful at the same time. A more serious barrier to even feeling very

Catholic in those days was the abortion issue. To me the Church's position was simply barbarous. When I wrote a pro-choice editorial for the faculty newspaper, I thought that my beliefs and those of the Church were irreconcilable.

And yet when the College of St. Benedict had a conference on ordaining women in 1974, I was eager to attend. Certainly a Church with women priests would be radically changed. The passion and eloquence of the speakers made an impression on me; I acknowledged that the Church I was detached from had as members women of great moral force. At the end of the conference, participants were asked to stand if they agreed with a statement that Catholic laywomen ought to begin calling for the ordination of women. I assumed every one in the auditorium would rise. I was shocked when I saw that only about a third of us were on our feet. Another embarrassing miscalculation, but this time I was not alone.

Recently I have been wondering what label fits me. If I say I am a "lapsed Catholic," I let the official Church define me. "Ex-Catholic" doesn't really fit, even though I believe in no Catholic dogmas, never attend Mass, and acknowledge no moral authority of popes or bishops. If neither belief nor practice makes me Catholic, why is it that I still *feel* Catholic? The hot air of male supremacist religion cannot fill me up again — what life remains? In the last year I have felt stirrings of spiritual renewal that I associate with Catholicism, not, I think, because that is my only context for spirituality but because my Catholic self, shadowy as it is, is fundamentally my spiritual self. At Quaker lesbian conferences I feel very Catholic when we sit in silence even though those silences are profoundly different from the silence at Mass, when I felt agitatedly unsure of what *ought* to be going on inside of me. Taking on a Catholic identification means that my Catholic past bears on my present and that I want to be fully aware of the links. My emotionally crippling Roman Catholic past needn't limit me now, and shutting it out of consciousness seems to work against recovery from pain. I call myself Catholic, then, on my own authority, acknowledging that I may not be free to do otherwise, the mould having been set so early.

I don't pray but I feel prayerful. Just knowing that some lesbians are struggling with the question of Catholic identity revives in me some old, deeply buried connections to

Catholicism. The inner calm I am beginning to find in meditation would not be so meaningful to me if I had no previous
spiritual training. Finally, feeling Catholic means I owe loyalty
to women working within the institutional Church, chiefly the
nuns of St. Scholastica Priory in Duluth who taught me for fifteen years. Scholars and artists as well as teachers, these women
had a profound influence on me. Leadership in the lesbian community was not their game plan for me, but they showed me that
a woman can be powerful and autonomous. I now regret that I
made fun of my college education in an essay I wrote ten years
ago, later published in *The Lesbian Path.* I couldn't then honor
my teachers and mentors as I now can, not in the way I was taught
to honor them, when I was young, as handmaidens of Jesus, but
in my own way, as sister travellers along a difficult path.

When I visited Picture Rocks, a retreat center in Arizona,
Sister Pat O'Donnell encouraged me to be as much or as little involved in the ritual life there as I chose to be but to feel free to
take communion. "It's your Church," she observed. And so it
is. When she was fired from her job for her part in breaking the
silence of *Lesbian Nuns,* I felt anger at my Church. I have a
fantasy that lesbian feminists will reconsecrate the ground
at Picture Rocks. Only our blessing can restore it to a holy
place.

Thanks partly to the spiritual renewal I experienced in the
desert, I was able to attend my father's funeral in a spirit of
peace and reconciliation. Before 1985, I would have seethed with
anger throughout the service, because a man was on the altar,
because my father always liked to cosy up to priests, because the
Church had nothing to offer a family riddled by alcoholism,
because priests and nuns got my mind early and bent it un-
naturally, and because Catholicism has meant to me the propa-
gation of fear and ignorance and the wielding of arbitrary
power. As it turned out, I felt none of those things and thus
could be open to the communal experience of celebrating a life
at its end. Catholicism has provided a structure for the enact-
ment of some healing rituals. And after the service, when the
priest acknowledged that my sister's eulogy had been more eloquent than his sermon, I loved the truth-telling of the moment.

Given my respect for lesbians and gay men who choose to express their Catholicism in traditional ways, I'm sorry to see the
anti-Catholic bias of the gay press. Partly this is an inheritance

from leftwing ideology. And partly it is prompted by the many acts of discrimination against homosexuals by the institutional Church. Certainly the gay press should point up the hypocrisy of the official Church stand on homosexuality and print information about maneuvers to block civil rights legislation on our behalf. But the cultural identity of Catholics ought to be respected in the gay press, just as the cultural identity of every other minority group is respected. Political points can be made about the oppressive Church without the accompanying assumption that anyone who considers herself both gay and Catholic is a fool.

I claim for myself the right to define what I mean by calling myself a Catholic lesbian. This is as fundamental to my freedom of speech as my right to call myself a lesbian. I still feel somewhat tentative about the identification "Catholic lesbian." I touch it as carefully as I touched the cactus around Picture Rocks.

For helping me think about this essay, I thank Matile Poor and Kathryn Strachota.

Curriculum Vitae

Hilda Hidalgo

In 1958 I was told I was "not qualified" to be served in a Texas diner. I had $50 in cash and $200 in travelers checks.

By that time I had left behind my aspirations to be a saint/martyr, clothed in nun's black, and succeeded in transforming myself into an assertive, sexual, joyful lesbian.

In 1960 I was told I was "not qualified" to sign a lease for an apartment in Newark, New Jersey. I had a permanent professional job and money to cover two months security.

Question: What is a saint?
Answer: A sensual, creative, industrious lesbian revolutionary who wants joy and fulfillment.

In 1962 I was told I was "not qualified" to be accepted at Rutgers Graduate School of Education. I had a B.A. cum laude, *an M.A. from an American university, and a combined average placing me in the top ten percent.*

I knew that it was impossible for me to develop a rational argument that would allow me to stay connected to the Catholic Church — the *summa cum non* of patriarchal institutions — while maintaining the integrity of my Puerto Rican lesbian persona. As a lesbian there is no room for me within the rigid, homophobic, sexist structure that is at the heart of institutional Catholicism.

In 1964 I was told I was "not qualified" to teach in Newark's public schools. I had a B.A. and an M.A. in Education, a permanent teacher's certificate from Puerto Rico and ten years of successful teaching experience.

I developed a spiritual/ethical system that incorporated many Catholic principles, particularly faith, hope and charity. Rebeling against racism, sexism, homophobia and the oppression of human beings are the acts of virtue that will earn me the right to Heaven. It is in these subversive and sometimes outrageous acts that I manifest the work and power of the Supreme Being within me.

In 1969 I was told I was "not qualified" to direct the guidance center at Livingston College, Rutgers University. I had an M.A. in Guidance and Counseling, an M.S.W. in clinical social work and more than five years of practical experience with individuals and groups.

Coming out in all spheres of my life — to family, friends, employers, working associates, the community at large — is practicing faith, hope and charity. These are acts of faith in myself and in my integrity; acts of faith in my fellow human beings, challenging them to honor the virtue of charity; acts of hope, risking survival in a homophobic society; acts of love, a "Magnificat" praising the Source of human diversity.

In 1976 I was told I was "not qualified" to be the Dean of the Rutgers School of Social Work. I had a Ph.D., held the rank of professor and had over fifteen years of administrative experience, five of them in academia.

In joining other community activists that form the body of my spiritual/ethical structure, we celebrate the Mass: a reenacting of our commitment as a collective body to the principles of justice and liberation. We honor the commandment to love others as we love ourselves, for there is no higher virtue.

In 1978 I was told I was "not qualified" to be president of a community college with a majority population of Hispanics. I was the first choice of the search committee after a two-year search and interviewing more than 60 candidates out of a pool of over 200.

> I am too brown to pass
> too outspoken to speak
> too oppressed to be docile
> too old to play games
> too woman to be a lady

Grace is still a force in my life. I find it in the caresses and understanding of my lover and lifetime mate, in communion with family and friends, in the enthusiasm that learning and discovery bring to my students, in the small but effective revolutionary acts I engage in with fellow community activists, and in walking tall and proud for I have nothing to hide, nothing to be ashamed of. And I sing to myself, Hail Hilda, you are full of grace being you — a Puerto Rican Lesbian Feminist!

As the Twig is Bent, the Tree's Inclined

Patricia Novotny

Late on a midsummer evening of my twelfth year I sat greedily devouring green apples and watching television. Both activities were mere distractions. I was in fact deeply concentrated on the contemplation of myself as sinner. Earlier that day I had failed in my resolution to forego the sins of impurity that had so dogged me since my first confession. Without them my list of sins was typically venial — lying, laziness, disrespect. But I understood a sin of impurity to be mortal, fatal to my soul. Throughout *The Beverly Hillbillies* and *Green Acres* I sat solemnly considering the consequences of my action. I distinctly remember thinking that if I died before reaching a confessional my soul would burn eternally in hell. And I remember being exquisitely happy.

It's true, my wickedness delighted me. The erotic games of childhood were interesting and often pleasurable in themselves. But that evening I realized, with no small perplexity, that I was as much enamored of being a bad girl, an outlaw. I reveled in my misery; I felt set apart and special. My concerns were monumental, not the trivial dalliances of my cohorts. (My fellow sinners were Protestant and whatever guilt they felt was, I think, free of considerations of mortality.) My guilt and trembling were somehow liberating. I had removed myself from God's judgment, being already condemned. I was suddenly beyond the pale, free for those eighteen or so hours before confession to commit any number of sins. That country beyond the pale was revealed to me as a rich, fascinating, if dangerous, landscape, where I could travel free of any authority but my own.

Thus ended my religious period. In competition with sexual urges and curiosity, God and my Catholicism had simply lost out. What I had so fervently believed suddenly lost its power. I sinned, I enjoyed sinning, and nothing happened to me as a consequence but pleasure. If I was to die and find myself in some improbable hell, well, it was worth it.

Fervent I had been. My father's family, which dominated our religious training, emigrated from Czechoslovakia in 1910 and brought with them a strictly dogmatic Catholicism. An already tight family budget was made all the tighter by my father's insistence that all the children attend Catholic schools, which the four of us did through high school. I don't really understand yet what a childhood without the landmarks of First Communion and Confirmation, the rituals of Lent, daily Mass, and votive candles, might have been like.

During my childhood the home of one of my aunts served as our family headquarters, suitably decorated in gaudy Catholic iconography — crucifixes, paintings, dried palms from the previous Easter season, rosaries hung on walls or arranged in piles around the room (convenient for those feeling an irresistible urge to pray); I was to discover that other homes had candy dishes in similar places. Each Sunday evening our family would travel from the city's newer neighborhoods to Aunt Mary's in South Omaha, home still to Sokol Hall and the Bohemian Cafe. We'd gather in the living room — grandmother, uncles, aunts, cousins, my parents and siblings — and pray the rosary together. My grandmother, though she lived fifty years in Nebraska, bitterly refused to learn English, so our recitations were a strange amalgam of English and Bohemian. Though I've forgotten all I knew of the language, I've retained an aptitude for the pronunciation — the insoluble imprint of a thousand murmured "Marias" and a fitting metaphor for my relationship to the Church.

After our prayers the food came out — sausages, freshly baked rolls and rye bread, pickled cabbage and cucumbers, wine and beer. Weddings and funerals were the same: a little solemnity followed by quantities of good food and plentiful drink, dancing and laughter. (My mother's family, dry-county Methodist farmers in Kansas, has left its own, albeit more subtle, mark upon me.)

I ate it all up — developing a fondness for food and for drink as well as an ardent religiosity. Like all children I was impressionable, and among the images around me in those early years

religious ones predominated. I can, for instance, recall my first
consciously sympathetic moment. Perhaps I was four or five,
pre-literate at any rate. Sitting in an overstuffed rocker, I paged
through a *Life* or *Look* magazine until coming upon a two-page
reprint of what must have been a Renaissance painting. I
remember fat babies, round mothers, well-muscled men. The
subject was the killing of the innocents ordered by a fearful
Herod, jealous of his power. I can still see the frightened eyes of
the children, the desperate poses of the mothers frozen in their
efforts to stop the soldier's sword from piercing their babies. I
began crying and continued for such a time and in such a
hysterical manner that my parents finally gave me a glass of wine
to calm me.

I don't think it's unusual for Catholic children to be devout.
Everyone tells of their plans to be nun or priest. Perhaps it is not
unusual to have planned, as I did, to be both — first nun, then
priest. Ultimately I hoped to be pope, but realized early that
some divine intercession would be necessary for such an achieve-
ment. During daily Mass at my grade school I would fantasize
being enveloped in a golden beam of light as I knelt at the communion rail. A deep, commanding voice — God's of course —
would fill the church and directly authorize my entrance into the
priesthood. Oh, I read comic books too and would fantasize
from them, and eventually I would read "adult" texts ever more
closely for hints of sexual activity — building blocks for my inci-
pient sexual imagination. But in my earliest years, religious
visions were the most compelling. I went through one particularly devout phase where I insisted upon dragging my mother
to Mass on Saturday morning, so I could congratulate myself
for my sacrifice (unmindful, apparently, of my mother's). I
must have been terribly obnoxious in my piety, as I probably am
still in the worst throes of my enthusiasms.

Devotion enjoyed its rewards. During that period I experienced a bona fide vision. Walking home from school one winter
afternoon, I realized I had forgotten my house key. As both my
parents worked and my older brothers were at that point in high
school or married, I knew I would be locked out. I had piano to
practice, school lessons to do, and wanted nothing more than to
be able to avoid spending the afternoon at a crabby neighbor's.
So I prayed. I struck some bargain — I'd do such and such if
you, Jesus, would get me into the house. Lo and behold, the side

door was unlocked, a truly uncharacteristic omission on the part of my cautious parents. I was pleased to get into the house (the only occasion I recall being eager to practice the piano), but I was exultant at being in direct two-way communication with the Son of God. The glow of privilege lingered for months.

I was a good kid, but I was not, despite my efforts, a saint. Still, nothing conflicted so early and directly with my religious beliefs as sex did. The information available to me regarding the early sexual experiences of others is too limited to provide a standard of measurement, so I don't know if I was always a sex maniac or only became one. I know we enjoyed in my neighborhood, among the girls and mostly boys of my approximate age, a fairly active curiosity. What amazes me most about those explorations are the elaborate fictions we concocted around them: doctors, of course, and spies, and robbers on the lam, cops on the make, Tarzans and Janes; nearly any model providing a pretextual power imbalance, an advantage, to force the issue of exposure. These were harmless games, I believe, except insofar as I felt guilt over them. And I agonized over the guilt. When I prepared to make my first confession, I searched frantically for the name I might give these sins in confessing them to the priest (how, I wonder, if they were not named did I know them as sins?). I remember being forced to ask my mother. Unable to face her as I did so, I stood behind the easy chair she sat in and spelled out "pulled down my pants." I think she had to look it up in my catechism. I wonder now how she kept a straight face.

Confessing a sin of impurity was like, if not exactly like, confessing any other sin. I don't recall the penitential burden being significantly greater, though I know I approached the confessional more apprehensively when I brought this particular sin to it. My apprehension increased dramatically after confessing to our new parish   pastor. An older, authoritarian man (who nearly bankrupted the parish with his extravagant building plans), Father M. was unwilling to pass over my sins of impurity with the same modesty as those before him. He interrogated me, inquiring after the precise circumstances of these sins in a degree of detail that was completely voyeuristic. It seemed to me that day that I spent years in the confessional and that the kneeler was covered with gravel. I left severely traumatized.

I didn't stop "sinning" as a result of that or other guilt-induced traumas; I simply stopped confessing. By high school I'd grown accustomed to living in a state of sin. I discovered sex and critical inquiry. With the latter I reformulated my beliefs and ethics to accommodate the former; that is, I invented my own religion. I renounced God and Catholicism and took to chasing girls. My insistent erotic impulse triggered a profound and far-reaching intellectual, political, and emotional awakening.

At thirty-two I remain an atheist (an agnostic whenever I board an airplane), but I am also — for better and worse — very much a Catholic. Yet the Catholic Church of my early training was not monolithic — it was comprised of a multiplicity of lessons and interpreters. From among them I retain certain, ineluctable habits of heart and mind. I belong to that pack of ex-Catholics running around with a capacity for awe and for worship and a tolerance for mystery that befuddle and sometimes annoy our Protestant fellow-travellers. My personal ethics and politics originate in the model of Christ, combined with the "love your neighbor" practical examples of my parents, particularly my mother. My father contributed, rather contributes, our continuing consciousness of the less fortunate (a sincere invocation during Grace before every meal). Christ as a teacher of love, peace, and nonviolence (teachings amplified by his modern disciples, Gandhi and King) retains a strong emotional and philosophical hold on me.

My early habituation to the Church's byzantine system of laws transferred easily to my study of our secular legal system. (Not to mention the uses to which I put my familiarity with Latin.) I remain haunted by the belief that I'm always being watched, but in my paranoia I've exchanged the CIA for God (and his pseudo-secular front man, Santa Claus). The certainty (or superstition?) that I will some day, some way, pay for my sins keeps me honest. Which means I retain some fear of divine or poetic justice and uncertainty about the difference between them.

Just as the Church left an impact on me so has my leaving the Church. Being forced to a choice between my feelings and church doctrine precipitated a thorough reversal of my worldview and left me with an abiding skepticism and mistrust of authority, however constituted. In politics and law both, my activities are limited to sporadic subversion (when I work in the law I practice on the lunatic fringe of public defense; my political activities are comprised of eclectic binges). I seem unable not only to participate fully in the establishment but in the anti-establishment as well, rejecting orthodoxies of any stripe. So I remain an outsider, the outlaw of my early years, with many of the same pleasures and costs. Which is, I realize, itself an orthodoxy of sorts.

I awoke during the middle of the night several days ago and wrote the following line: "He does not worry about the dangers of the road. He is on his way to church." In the absence of faith I have perhaps made a virtue of those dangers, sometimes reflexively rejecting the safety of not only the Church but numerous other institutions. But so long as gay people are defined as outlaws we must forego the tenuous security of a respectable, imitative homosexuality. We must not mistake the consolation prizes of fickle political patronage and liberal solicitude for the unqualified, inalienable (if you will) securing of our human rights.

Finally, there is no finally. In the absence of faith all is change, relativity, merely mortal efforts at understanding. Still, it's a beautiful day and for now that's enough.

The Ironic Legacy of Sister Mary Educator

Joanne M. Still

When I was a Catholic high school student in the 1960s, I had this fantasy that somewhere along the boardwalk in a New Jersey seashore resort there was this baseball-throwing game called "Bean-a-Nun." For a quarter, you got three baseballs to throw at a procession of Styrofoam nunheads. If you hit one, you didn't have to go to Mass for a month. If you hit two, you won two years' good behavior time off of Purgatory. Three out of three won you parental permission to go to public school.

I never found my fantasy boardwalk booth. I went to Mass at the required times, and I graduated from a Catholic high school. I no longer believe in Purgatory, and if there really is such a place, I'll be damned. Literally, I'm told. And now I have a different fantasy: I see myself talking to Sister Mary Educator, a black-and-white composite image of all the nuns who ever made me cower in a classroom during my 13 years of Catholic school education. I tell her about the legacy she left me — some of it bitter, none of it sweet, and much of it ironic. (Telling her isn't as much fun as tossing a baseball, but the beaning is more effective.)

First, the Legacy of the Bitter — Sister Mary Educator's bequest of moral, ethical, and/or philosophical pronouncements. For at least a short time, at some point, I believed all of them were higher truths that were as gifts, to be treasured and embraced. At some other point, I discovered them to be lies or, at best, half-truths. These "rules to live by" could have ruined my life. The bitterness comes from my discovery that the neat little formula for eternal happiness was fraught with equations that just didn't add up when one factored in a variable called "The Real World."

Further study beyond Sister's classroom and a healthy dose of Elixir of Life Experience have helped me to factor in said variable, and to fill in the other halves of those half-truths. To illustrate:

•Confession is good for the soul...but when dealing with traffic cops who claim they've caught you speeding, it is good for a summons.

•Swearing, cursing, and using filthy language is a sign that a person is ignorant and has a limited vocabulary...unless the person is able to use such language in new and interesting ways, and then it is a sign of creativity and wit.

•Entertaining impure thoughts is as sinful as doing impure things...but doing "impure" things is much more entertaining, and saves countless dollars on psychotherapy.

•The Pope is the Vicar of Christ on Earth...and if this is true, Christ must have left a note instructing Peter and his successors to gather artifacts that would become known as "the Vatican treasures"; the reason behind this directive is lost to us forever, the original document no doubt having gone the way of other bits of interesting papyrus during one of the meetings of the Council of Nicea.

•The Bible is the inspired word of God...but God, inspired as He may have been, was a writer, not an editor; God's early drafts are lost to us forever.

•Charity begins at home...but is not tax-deductible — charity *really* begins at the United Way.

•The Pope is infallible in matters of faith...in matter of fact, the *reason* we know the Pope is infallible is that a Pope woke up one morning and declared he was, and since he was now infallible, no one could say he wasn't; people who are not Pope who claim such omniscience have no friends, and are usually unemployable.

•Things that The Faithful believe that cannot be explained are called Mysteries...how the remaining Faithful can believe that the Church is entitled to own a large piece of Manhattan, tax-free, is inexplicable, and very Mysterious indeed.

Please don't misunderstand. I am grateful for what Sister Mary Educator bequeathed to me by way of these pronouncements, and by way of everything else I learned while I was in her care. That's the irony: Sister taught me things beyond what she intended to teach, and gave me things beyond what she intended to give.

Oh, there were the usual academic subjects, of course, things she taught that were gifts of knowledge, though many of these proved to be useless in real life. (I can't even remember the last time I had to calculate the area of a scalene triangle, and most of the friends with whom I conversed in classical Latin are no longer in my social circle.) Sister always taught, though, that the reason for studying these topics was to learn to think. She insisted that I not just accept what I read in books, but that on my own I observe, listen, question, and debate, explore, consider, and reason. She assumed that after I completed these exercises, I would arrive at the proper conclusions. My conclusions turned out to be *improper,* however, and I attribute this mostly to the fact that I practiced the aforementioned mental gymnastics on *her.*

It would have made her wimple limp to know just how I was applying her lessons, but fortunately for her (because I disliked her enough to enlighten her), I wasn't aware of this either as it was happening. In retrospect, the truth can be told.

Sister was a strong woman, the personification of "authority" in my world. Though she tried to instill respect — even awesome respect — for the parish patriarchy, it was quite clear to me that it was really Sister who ran the show. Through her, I had my first taste of woman-power. And I saw that it was good.

I also observed that Sister had had a fine education. I was not aware that some people didn't think this was a good thing for the rest of womankind. Sister wasn't aware of this either, or else she just forgot to mention it. But I saw that Sister *knew* really interesting things — about physics and geography, Chaucer and Chardin, the funeral rites of Neanderthals, the theories of Freud (even if he *was* dirty), and about mixing liquids in a test tube that made the chemistry lab smell like a stable on a hot day.

Sister also didn't mention that certain wannabees (as in, "when I grow up I wannabe...") were considered by many in the outside world to be more appropriate as male aspirations. As a result, many of my former schoolmates are now reported to be doing awfully unfeminine things, such as running corporations (or worse, starting them), practicing law and medicine, and constructing buildings. I hear we also have a few musicians. I guess some of us took her seriously when she said we were supposed to discover our talents, develop them, and use them, whatever they were.

And Sister supplied a living answer to my questions about the popular notion that a woman needs a man in her life in order to function. Except for a priest to say Mass and listen to her sins against charity, Sister Mary Educator obviously got along just fine without a man. She had other women she depended on for both her livelihood and her creature comforts. The order (headed by someone's mother, but I forget whose) employed her, and at home, Sister Laundress, Sister Housekeeper, and Sister Cook kept the hearth warm for when Sister Mary Educator came back after a hard day at the blackboard.

Sister did everything with steel-spined certainty — and she encouraged in her students such ·qualities as independence, leadership, and self-pride. I'm sure it never occurred to her that displays of such behavior were obstacles to the development of the mindless complacency so necessary for a smooth ride through adult womanhood outside the convent.

Sister thought it was a really swell idea to keep girls separated from boys during the crucial adolescent years. She reasoned that boys would present a distraction in the classroom, an interference in our pursuit of academic excellence. Thus, as a young woman I was bathed in the glow of woman-brightness, and I had the opportunity to view, undiluted, woman-intellect.

It is largely because of Sister Mary Educator that I am an ex-Catholic, a semi-liberal, a free-spirited soul, an entrepreneur, and proud of all that I am — including the fact that I am a vocal, out-of-the-closet, dyed-in-the-school-uniform-wool Lesbian. I would have been all of those things, no doubt, if I had never known her, but I might not have accepted being all those things so readily, so joyously, or so young.

Sister Mary Educator lived in bondage, her life dedicated to serving the Catholic patriarchy, but it was her duty to teach. That she taught me how to be free is perhaps the greatest irony of all.

My Wagon of Collectibles

Mab Maher

Some years ago my uncle Charley, a survivor of San Francisco's great earthquake, led me along the route that as a child he took with his family to escape the raging fires which followed the quake. We walked from his childhood home in the Mission District to a spot on Twin Peaks. I was amazed at the sharpness of detail he still had about this trip of many decades before. He remembered where he turned corners, where he saw friends branch off in other directions, and where he lost things from his red wagon, half-filled with toys and half-filled with household items. He survived and the details of that survival were keenly available in his mind.

Ten years ago at the age of 41, I left the convent and Church and, like my uncle Charley, I left with little externally to take along — for the journey "out" was swift, in personal and emotional survival. Only lately have I begun to assess what I took along, what was in "my wagon" as I avoided disaster.

Often when I hear myself described as a "raised Catholic lesbian," I wince. I try to believe that my Catholic past is just that — past. I do not wish to deal with it. Yet I know that I am increasingly aware of how I survived that strenuous journey from being a raised Catholic to being a nun of 18 years to opening to my lesbian identity. Like uncle Charley, I am learning to remember each turn I took, what I lost — friends or family respect or securities that once came with orthodox Catholic belief.

I seldom wince when the Catholic Church is roundly criticized in feminist circles. Often I join or initiate such criticism. I read Mary Daly's insightful analysis of Christianity with the zeal of a new hunter out to get an old prey and, at the same time, disagree with the totality of her condemnation. I often turn aside when other feminists dare to mention that they "still" belong to the

Church. But I refuse to hear sharp depreciation of my parents' religious beliefs. Since their deaths, I have come to appreciate that how they lived was within the boundaries of their cultural and emotional possibilities. Though certainly inadequate, *something* is to be said for the old truism, "they did the best they could under those circumstances."

Rarely do I ask questions about restoration of anything valuable from my Catholic history. Yet I know myself to be moderately honest about my experience and I am sometimes faced with this question: What was there to keep me in the Church so long? Easy answers are fear, security, and the belief that I could do some good for others. Others are my inability to deal for so long with my lesbian identity, the excitement of a good education and the women friends I truly cherished.

But why *did* I stay so long and was there anything in that time which translates into my present life as a lesbian and, if so, what?

As I have pondered this question, I continually come up with the fact that what is valuable to me now has often been learned by opposing the Church or letting go of it, and by changing my mind — literally. It is almost as if by being such a foe to me, the Church has allowed me to see into the nature of patriarchy in stark ways. I have been shocked at how deeply patriarchal I was, even when I thought I was living in a matriarchy, the convent. I feel embarrassed when I recall that I once used "her" and "she" to refer to the Church.

My own coming out as lesbian has been the keenest antithesis to what I was taught as a Catholic, for the Church, as I knew it, was most punitive to sexual life expressions other than hetero-sexuality and chastity. I am able now to see certain things characteristic of my Catholic history since I have acted over and against its teaching on sexuality. Every lesbian's experience of the Church differs, even while we unfortunately hold in com-mon the oppression, sexual, social and economic, which as women we have suffered there. I would say that my Catholic history was liberal, non-fundamentalist and, because of the education I had in theology in the 1960's, intellectually creative — or as a friend puts it, "You were a spiritual lefty." I am aware that this tendency in me to liberalism is the great temptation to avoid being radical. I believe that all too often liberal causes in the Church detour from the essential task of examining systematic patriarchy which underlies all.

I believe what remains for me — in my wagon of collectibles — are three attitudes of soul which I still find worth refining in my alchemical pot of experience. These three attitudes of soul are: a belief that what is truly radical is complex; an active hope for justice toward all species on Earth; and a deep love and respect for women seeking to be free. Those of you who have studied the *Baltimore Catechism* may humorously note that these three, as I have presented them, are also the names of the "theological virtues." They are now, however, the fruit of my experience and struggle and do not come from any metaphysical revelation outside myself. My faith, hope and love are feminist.

A Belief That What Is Truly Radical Is Complex

Adrienne Rich in a 1977 speech/essay spoke of the need for us lesbians to make "connections which demand of us, not only pride, anger and courage, but the willingness to think and face our own complexity."[1] Later in the same essay, she urged lesbians to avoid the temptation to "sterile 'correctness' [leading] into powerlessness, an escape from radical complexity."[2] My own feminist journey has kept me close to complexity. I do not mean mystification, the process so familiar to patriarchy in which obscurity is confused with the sacred — "We can't understand it; it is mystery," etc. By "complexity" I mean that I don't get the inner sources and understandings of issues other than at the intuitive level. I believe in mystery, not mystification. For example, it is a mystery to me why I am a lesbian; I just am.

As I say that I believe what is radical is complex, at the same time, I also say that, because of this complexity, my action must be simple. As in alchemy, the vessel must be simple to accommodate the transformation process in it.

As I write this, I am involved in the 1985 controversy among us feminists and lesbians over the nature and legality of pornography. My deepest worry about this struggle is that we will simplify very complex issues before we have the hard and patient dialogue from which some resolution can come. And in this case, our appeal to the law, that most patriarchal of institutions, will become the high-priest simplifier.

My own experience of myself has been that I am very much a creature of benign and violent forces. I know that the violence I have felt in loss and separation of friends and lovers can be interpreted as something I have internalized from patriarchy. I am sure that is partially true. But I also know that in myself I carry propensities for ill will and harm, as well as for compassion and grandeur. In Jungian terms, that means I have experienced my "shadow side." Often in lesbian gatherings I feel most uncomfortable when we present ourselves as totally innocent victims of patriarchy, as if all that is wrong and oppressive comes from outside ourselves. Surely, oppression is a complex issue and one that I deal with in myself daily and when doing therapy with women. It has been very destructive for us women to believe in our sweet goodness — either as virgin or mother, as the Church puts it. These are outside models of femininity which are really conformity to male norms. That is clear. But I also believe that somehow what is equally dangerous to us as lesbians is a neo-Puritanism, a correctness without compassion, a making of present consciousness and its implications absolute norms for time ahead and time past. My own experience with alcoholic recovery and sobriety makes it very clear to me that life is an admixture of the forces of healing and destruction. As writer Jan Clausen aptly puts it:

> ...I want fiction [life] that, while reflecting the simplest, most profoundly political laws of social life (oppression and injustice breed resistance, for example), at the same time leaves room for ambiguity and the way people have of being so often both worse and better than they ought to be.[3]

I would often like to believe that all that is lacking in me has been the result of what was outside-in taught me and then return it to the doorstep of patriarchy. But the truth of my experience is that I am responsible for the ill-will, chaos and division which I evoke. Perhaps what I long for most in lesbian feminist circles is our growing understanding of the forces inside us as women, both those affirming life and those inviting emotional death. We need to know, I believe, both what oppresses us from without and from within. We have done fine analysis from without, but, I believe, we have not yet asked in sufficient depth what lies in our own hearts, what is in the heart of womankind. I believe we are seeing this depth unfold as it is increasingly portrayed in our fiction, such as Clausen's, before we can begin to formulate it theoretically (if the latter is even desirable).

I believe that having been raised Catholic has had a good deal to do with my questioning and search in this area. Being Catholic always meant, if nothing else, that I was not simply a product of behavior. Such concepts as soul, immortality, evil, and mysticism often came up. I am reinterpreting these within my own life experience as lesbian. It is not enough for me now as a lesbian feminist to be considered only a product of my own behavior. Considerations of soul, mystery, and the complexity of human imagination are deeply embedded in me from Catholicism and, even if that were not so, I wish to keep them around.

An Active Hope for Justice Toward All Species on Earth

When a Catholic, I had great love for Francis of Assisi. I still do. I went to Assisi, to Mount LaVerna, that mountain given to Francis. Italian lore has it that persons who go to that sacred place are radically changed. Ironical as it may seem, it was on that mountain that I, then 31 years old, first let in (but briefly) my being lesbian. I cannot explain that nor do I even seek to. Yet there has been and continues to be in me a great love for this man whose ideology led him to biocentric (life-centered) sharing among all species over homocentric (human-centered) arrogance, the belief that we are better than other species. However he interpreted the Christian gospels, it did come out that he believed other species had as much right to the gift of life as humans. Birds, nature, the elements were connected for him in deeply mystical ways, in the common "peace" that all deserved. Francis of Assisi has been for me my only strong link back into Christian awareness. Perhaps at deep levels I do believe that the gospel of the Christ figure has been grossly misinterpreted by patriarchy — as have been the lives of women — and, for whatever reasons, Francis seemed to go through some wide tunnel of awareness to big consciousness among the interface of all aspects of life, even back there in the 13th century.

Being "raised Catholic" is, of course, not the same at all as coming to terms with understanding how to live the gospel. I ask as I write this what would it be like if I were called a "gospel raised lesbian." I believe that if the true meanings of the gospel had been lived, my being lesbian would have been supported from early childhood. The problem with the word "gospel," as it is commonly used, is that it seldom carries more than the speaker's projections onto it — all too often it is reduced to emotional fundamentalism romanticized into transcendent belief. The implications of the gospel and its beatitudes in life are profound. For myself, I cannot be sure how deeply informed my own "coming out" process was by them, but, at some point, I began to do justice to myself. I began to internalize the need to feed, clothe, and be merciful to my own being. And I believe that the ultimate justice is to remember who we are and to live in that remembrance.

A Deep Love and Respect for Women Seeking to Be Free

As I look back, I see that one impelling motivation for my entering the convent at 20 was to be with women and not to have to deal with fitting the expected model of marriage. In my years as a nun, I grew in a deep love and respect for the struggle of women to be free. Granted, that struggle was sometimes incredibly unconscious, subservient to male authority and powerless to effect much change in the overall institutional Church. Yet many women in the community to which I belonged were activists for justice and peace. Their political and social sense, motivated in them by the Christian beatitudes, has remained in my life. I myself was active one year for the medical rights of farm workers in the Rio Valley in Texas, and another summer worked in New York City at the *Catholic Worker*.

I believe that often I, when a woman in the Church, was more deeply motivated by the suffering of others than by my own. That is, often my action for justice for the disinherited ones of the earth simply hid my own oppressed state. Yet misogyny has made all of us women in the institutional Church disinherited pilgrims. When the pain of my oppression became intolerable, I began to see what I did not like to see: that I was compliant with the victimization I was undergoing. Often I am impatient with those in the Church who do not take on the task of resisting their own oppression, especially lesbians who live silently in the Church without any protest for the silencing of their rights. Further, I rage at those whose placebo (for themselves, not me) is to offer pastoral care *at* me, rather than admit the integrity of my lesbian decision.

Remembering How to Remember

I am aware that as I have used the word "history" throughout this essay it means remembrance more than selection of events. I am fond of Barbara Deming's verse lines: "I must undress down to the bone, take all the/ pictures off the wall/ and remember who I am." *The Anamnesis*, a prayer in the Eucharistic service recalling the final events in the life of Christ, is a remembering but it is also a representation of those events in the present moment. In many ways, real remembering is letting the past live in the present.

As a raised Catholic lesbian, remembrance is often painful. It is like the walk I took with my uncle Charley. And those walks which are memories of the devastation intended us, but which we survived, are testimonies to our strength. They help us to remember how to remember what lies in the heart of life, far below institutional systems of any sort.

1. "The Meaning of Our Love for Women," in *On Lies, Secrets, and Silence.* New York: Norton and Co., 1979, pp. 223-34.

2. *Ibid.,* p. 227.

3. "Books and Life: On the Political Morality of Fiction," *Off Our Backs*, July 1985, p. 19.

Letter To My Children

Barbara Zanotti

My dearest children,

So many times over the past eleven years we touched on the story of our separation; of how it came to be that you live with your father, and I live with and love a woman. So often I have tried to tell the story, but always fumbled with words, stumbling to give language to feelings that are a powerful mix of grief and joy. When I began to put this book together I knew I wanted to write about us and the road we have walked down together. I felt deeply that the geography of our lives could best be explored within a discussion of faith and integrity.

The roots of our situation are found in my own childhood. I lived in an unpredictable world of fear and loneliness. When I discovered God I dug my roots deep in His presence. He became a loving father who knew every hair on my head, a faithful friend whose love I felt in the world around me. In turn, all of my feelings — sensual, emotional, intellectual, physical — were directed toward loving God. Daily Mass, devotional reading, prayer and personal sacrifice, all were part of loving God and giving thanks for the blessings of His presence and faithfulness to me. As I look back on my childhood, two truths become very apparent: the first is that religious faith helped me survive, and the second that I learned to equate love with pleasing others and sacrificing myself for them. Religion turned me to God and away from myself.

In a Catholic school setting these dispositions were complicated by teachings on sin and holiness which left me feeling guilty, anxious and unworthy. On the one hand, God loved me; on the other, I was a sinner entirely undeserving of love. These were confusing matters for my eight-year-old mind and heart. Today, I still feel traces of the inner tensions of those years in my personal struggle with assertiveness.

But my school years also included warm, gentle moments. I remember with great fondness my feelings of attraction to, and comfort with, the sisters whom I honored. I especially recall pleasant summer afternoons when I walked the hot mile to my piano lesson and passed through the convent garden. I still see the sisters sitting in the clear light, each engaged in needlework, talking with one another. I hear them say hello to me, and feel again the pleasure and awkwardness of those moments. Feelings of peace rise within me as I remember those afternoons. Then, I could only imagine their love for God; now, as a lesbian woman, I can imagine their love for each other.

When I became a teenager at a girls' Catholic high school, I looked forward to reading *The Imitation of Christ* at recess while other girls talked about boys. I wanted to be a nun and to deepen my intimacy with God. The few boys I dated couldn't measure up to God — and besides I was bewildered about sex and disconnected from my sexual feelings. Given your own vital self-awareness, I expect that this is hard for you to understand. But I lived in a very enclosed Catholic mental world guided by institutional authority and established rules.

In August 1958 I entered the Notre Dame Convent with only one desire: to give myself to God. Scattered on my desk now as I write you are pages of a journal I kept for the three years I remained. The entries alternate between love, grief and resignation. The life I had longed for turned out to be full of difficulties for me. We were instructed never to question authority, to seek suffering and rejection, and to conform our lives to the crucified Christ. In those days these attitudes were considered the very essence of holiness. I had known this from childhood, but in the convent I found the practice of obedience a source of great anxiety, and the mandate against friendship simply inexplicable. I remember kneeling in the chapel contemplating the figures of Christ and John at the Last Supper, sensing their love for each other and the blessedness of their intimacy. For almost three years I struggled with loneliness and anxiety, praying for an inner peace that never came. In the end, I sadly took off my habit in a tiny corner room.

In shock and bewilderment I returned to the world. The novice mistress, whose letter I now hold in my hand, wrote that "God has other plans for you. Trust Him." The trauma of leav-

ing generated a kind of mental cataclysm. I sought the help of a
psychiatrist who analyzed me as having suppressed sexual needs.
"Get married," he said, "and you'll be fine." And so it was that
when I met your father, a likable, good-natured man, marriage
seemed predestined.

I remember a retreat I made just prior to our marriage. The
retreat director spoke of the family as a reflection of the Trinity.
He preached that the fulfillment of woman was in wifely submis-
sion and motherhood. He urged us to contemplate Mary at the
foot of the cross and to find in her suffering the strength to endure our own sorrow. We were told that our bodies were a
chalice to receive the seed of man, that our arms were altars on
which our children could rest. Fifty young women considering
marriage attended that retreat. None of us spoke with one
another. None of us questioned the ethic of sacrifice that was offered to us. It was as familiar as communion bread.

I want you to know this because those religious feelings had
everything to do with my intention when I married your father.
They were the commitments that shaped the first six years of our
marriage. With great enthusiasm I developed family religious
rituals, meal-time prayers, and various holy day customs. I gave
myself completely to serving the needs of your father, and you
children as you came along. Maybe David and Stephen can
remember my blessing them at night, or being brought to
church, or hearing stories about God's love. I was creating a
strong Catholic family and fulfilling God's will. And then Susan
died.

You asked me to tell you about her so many times, and I did.
How she was born with a weak heart that could not sustain her
fragile life; how she died ten days after her birth. We've visited
her grave together. Do you remember?

Your father said I was never the same after that; he was right.
In my inability to grieve for her I confronted my own numbness.
No tears. No rage. Nothing. I had a dream shortly after her
death in which I died and was condemned to hell — because I
was not real. This new and very disturbing awareness was a profound shock, a painful first nudge towards personal honesty and
liberation. To resolve this dilemma of self-alienation I began to
explore the terrain of my own feelings. Slowly I set aside rules
and laws and realized for the first time the deep inadequacy of
living according to reason and will.

Seeking interests outside our home I embarked on a program of teaching and study that brought some measure of satisfaction, but also family strains. Your father missed the carefully tended home, the cozy smells of home-cooking, and my reliable presence. As I became politicized by the anti-war movement and the Black struggle for civil rights, our political differences increased the tension. While he celebrated the American way and traditional family values, I began to understand political and economic systems of oppression. I remember the afternoon when I stood in the sun porch, picked up my copy of *Sisterhood is Powerful*, and read the words of women claiming freedom. Terrified, I put the book down. Here were words for my feelings. Here were other women who felt as I did. Your father and I were on a collision course.

On the one hand I felt some exhilaration in searching out the meaning of things on my own terms, but on the other I could see the wrenching consequences of my searching on your life. By this time, Carolyn and Elizabeth were born. I was juggling internal chaos with some modicum of external calm. I tried to shore up family life with folk Masses in our dining room. Father Bill and Sister Kathy became a part of the wider family circle and their presence helped me to hold things together for a while. Inwardly, I felt alone, isolated and terribly frightened, seeing no way to resolve the conflict without enormous suffering. I began to sleep on the couch, finding great comfort in a bed of my own. In prayer I invoked the God of liberation for wisdom and strength, writing in my journal: "The word of God to people is always to remain open, to let go of anything that holds one back from being fully human."

I became depressed, weepy, and listless. Your father and I sought counseling help, a process which helped me to accept my own feelings. I was finally able to admit to myself the deep alienation I had felt in our sexual life, and the absence of intimacy that rendered our marriage lifeless. By this time, family life was filled with arguments between your father and me. You probably remember how awful it was. After a wrenching process, I decided to divorce your father. What the future held was uncertain, yet I was sure that I could not remain his wife. But the decision about your care was the hardest decision of all.

We all stood in the kitchen that fateful winter afternoon. I began to talk about divorce. David and Stephen began to cry. I tried to assure you of my love, but you felt what was really happening: family life was drastically changing and Mom wasn't going to be around. In a flash I remembered all the wonderful times we had shared. How I liked to take Stephen to the kitchen window to watch the sunset. How I delighted in the warmth of David's hand as we trekked through the woods behind the house. How we piled Carolyn into the toddler jumper and enjoyed her playfulness as she swayed back and forth. How we gathered around Elizabeth in her baby seat to sing sweet lullabyes. All that was changing for me, too. I could scarcely hold myself together, with all these memories rushing in on me, but I could see no other way. I knew in my heart that I was unable to be a full-time parent. I felt literally uncreated. Without myself I had little to offer you. For his part, your father welcomed the task of everyday parenting.

We all made the painful transition. You to a household with Dad and a housekeeper, me to a tumultuous journey of self-discovery. I felt torn by guilt and shame; some family members rejected me, most old friends ignored me. I knew that their disapproval of me broke the circle of love around you and this grieved me enormously. The early years of our living apart were especially difficult. Sometimes our visits were loving and intimate, other times you felt the freedom to rage against me. In this desperate transition I felt sustained by religious faith. I wrote in my journal, "I experience being held by a Power greater than myself. Only this comforts me through these terrible days. I must have faith and create meaning."

I focused on work and joined with the Catholic left in a variety of political struggles. I tried to make my work seem important to you in the hope of justifying my absence from the household. What you thought and felt was so important to me. Sometimes, looking back, I recall only problems, but there were also many happy times: Carolyn and I swimming in the waves at Singing Beach; Elizabeth's sixth birthday party at the mobilization office; celebrating with Stephen at the Boston Pops; watching and listening to David play his trombone with the Weymouth town band. What happy moments come to your mind?

During the third year of our living apart I began to be aware of my feelings for women. Very slowly I let my needs for intimacy come to the surface. On the day I said out loud, "I am a lesbian," I felt an enormous sense of liberation, integration, and personal power. I wrote about the process this way, "My ache was for communion of mind, spirit, flesh — a relationship in which I could be myself at last." Peeling back all the old definitions, setting aside all the old authorities, I came to consciousness as a lesbian feminist woman, finding myself outside everything I thought was true, and searching for other women with whom I could create new paths defined by our own words.

I like to think that our relationship improved as I achieved some measure of pleasure and integrity in my own life. Just as I saw you grow up, you witnessed steady changes in me. I remember when you boys asked me if I wanted a tie for Christmas. Aha, they suspect, I thought. I know it was more difficult for you, dear daughters, so your friendship with my lover, your thoughtfulness toward her, and your delightful participation in our life together is a deep gift to me.

Things have turned out so differently than I expected. I wanted to provide you with a rich religious heritage because I knew from my own experience how sustaining faith can be. But when I felt the weight of patriarchy within Christianity, and identified the misogyny that pervades the tradition, the entire system gradually eroded and ultimately the symbols collapsed, unable to mediate meaning. I suffered the loss of God and began to plough a spiritual land I could call my own.

And so, when you ask me if I believe in God, I draw a deep breath. I start to say, "It all depends on what you mean by god," and you, in frustration, shrug your shoulders and say, "Ma, just tell us if you believe in God." And so I say, "No, if what you mean is a supernatural being who rules the world, but yes, if you mean the Essence which unites us with one another, the Holy Communion we create through our love, the Strength we experience in striving to birth a feminist world." When I begin to speak in female imagery you become quickly embarrassed, but I want you to know how my lesbian existence led me to Changing Woman, Spider Grandmother, Old Woman — She who is known by many names; She who is the Source of all. My hope is that you find Her, too.

The security I set out to give you turned out to be a difficult and often painful childhood with a live-away lesbian mother and a landscape of religious questions. Each of you has emerged from this complex cocoon with goodness, courage and a

generous openness to life. I thank you deeply for all you bring to
me. What I am trying to bequeath to you is still in the making.

My love to you,
Mom

Biographical Notes

Gloria Evangelina Anzaldúa is a Chicana tejana lesbian from South Texas. The land, *lo mejicano,* and her indigenous roots inspirit her work as does a sense of *comunidad* with all marginal people, especially lesbians and women of color. She is co-editor of *This Bridge Called My Back: Writing by Radical Women of Color* and is a contributing editor to *Sinister Wisdom.* Her work has appeared in *Cuentos: Stories by Latinas, IKON, Conditions,* and *Third Woman. Borderlands,* a collection of her poetry, will be published by Spinsters/Aunt Lute Press in Spring of 1987. She is currently teaching creative writing at Vermont College and a workshop called Women's Voices at UC Santa Cruz.

Martha Courtot was born in Cincinnati in 1941, her father a taxi driver, her mother a beautician. Her earliest memory is being awake in a room full of sleepers. She has had three daughters who have taught her. With a B.A. from Seton Hall, she is currently working on her Master's. Sometimes she would like to fall into sleep, breathing in the comforting warmth of others but she seems to have an imperative for waking. She is working class, fat, intellectual and a poet.

Margaret Cruikshank is a teacher and writer who lives in San Francisco. Although she misses her native Minnesota, she's a zealous convert to California hedonism and self-improvement. She edited *Lesbian Studies, New Lesbian Writing* and *The Lesbian Path.* She attended Catholic schools for twenty-two years, finally wresting a Ph.D. from the Jesuits at Loyola.

M. Cunningham was born a Gemini in 1947. True to her sign she has suffered repeated identity crises throughout her life, beginning with her age four determination not to wear a "cow girl" outfit, insisting instead on her own Hopalong Cassidy gear. She attended Catholic elementary school, public high school, public college, and several private and public graduate schools. She holds a B.A. and M.A. in history and has taught on the junior college, secondary, and elementary school levels. She was married at the age of twenty-three, came out to herself at the age of thirty-five, and divorced at the age of thirty-seven. There were no children. On occasion she has been known to paint, read compulsively, write, scuba dive, backpack, and eat junk food. At the moment she is trying to quit smoking for the second time. She loves dogs (dislikes cats, unfortunately) and is currently hoping to get a new cocker spaniel puppy. She and her lover live (more or less) very happily in a large Metropolitan area in the United States.

Jennifer DiCarlo is a lesbian writer on a journey.

Karen Doherty was born in Elizabeth, New Jersey in 1952. She graduated from Trinity College in Washington, DC and now lives in Manhattan. Her most piercing religious insight came at age 11 when she was asked to name the two kinds of sin. "Moral and Venereal," she answered promptly. Not the answer Sister had on her paper, but nonetheless still probably true.

Hilda Hidalgo is a professor of social work and public administration of the Faculty of Arts and Sciences at Rutgers University. She has published research on Puerto Rican Lesbians, and was one of the editors and contributors to the National Association of Social Work's publication *Lesbian and Gay Issues: A Resource Manual for Social Workers.* She was selected in 1984 by the *Ladies Home Journal* as one of Fifty American Heroines, the Heroine for the State of New Jersey, A Master in Education.

Lorna Hochstein is a former religious studies educator. She recently received a doctorate in pastoral psychology and works in private practice as a pastoral psychotherapist. Her special area of interest is the effect of organized religion on lesbians and, more important, the effect of lesbian feminist spirituality on organized religion and on practitioners of organized religion.

Mary E. Hunt, co-founder and director of WATER (Women's Alliance for Theology, Ethics and Ritual), holds a Doctorate in Philosophical and Systematic Theology from the Graduate Theological Union, Berkeley, California. She has served as instructor of ethics at Wesley Theological Seminary (Washington, DC) and a Visiting Professor of Theology at ISEDET, an ecumenical seminary in Buenos Aires. She is a frequent lecturer at academic institutions, and has authored a wide range of feminist theological essays. Dr. Hunt is currently at work on *Fierce Tenderness: Toward a Feminist Theology of Friendship.*

Altogracia Pérez Maceira was born in New York City. Her father is from the Dominican Republic and her mother, who raised her, is Puerto Rican. She was raised in a welfare household in the South Bronx where she presently works. She is completing her second theological degree because, in spite of the Church's many negative aspects, it has been an important source of power for her and her people. She still believes it is worth struggling to re-call and re-claim the prophetic tradition that is part of the Christian tradition.

Mab Maher is a writer and transpersonal psychologist-teacher in San Francisco.

Linda Marie is a writer who has been published in many women's newsletters and magazines. She is the author of a novel, *I Must Not Rock*; and a short story included in the collection *True To Life Adventure Stories* (Vol. II), edited by Judy Grahn. The latter has been made into a dramatic reading. She makes her home in San Francisco.

Mary Mendola is a survivor. She is a U.S. Army veteran of the Viet Nam era, an ex-Maryknoll nun, a bureaucrat, a videotape writer and producer, an anarchist and patriot, a corporate vice president in the television industry — and, a gardener in Brooklyn. She has been a gay activist since the early 80's, has appeared on both radio and television talk shows, and is a frequent speaker at both local and national meetings of gay organizations. She is the author of *Voice From The Cement Desert* (Helios Book Publishing Company, 1972); and, *The Mendola Report: A New Look At Gay Couples* (Crown Publishing Compnay, 1980).

Kathleen Meyer is forty-four years old and spent nearly twenty-four of those years in the convent. During the past two years she has enjoyed a warm "home life" with Lora and a rewarding teaching career as an adult educator in the Los Angeles Unified School District. She is also a staff member of the Peace and Justice Center of Southern California. She is a member of the Conference for Catholic Lesbians, and is presently looking into the possibilities of doing hospice work with women who have contracted AIDS.

Mev Miller (aka Mary Evelyn Miller) lives in New Haven and works for a distributor of small, alternative press books. She also works at Bloodroot, a feminist vegetarian restaurant and bookstore. Her political work is done in association with a women's affinity group, Spinsters Opposed to Nuclear Genocide (a specific name with a broad focus). In addition, she is a singer/guitarist who writes and performs her own work.

Valerie Miner's novels include *Winter's Edge, Blood Sisters, Movement* and *Murder in the English Department.* Her widely translated and published fiction focuses on cross-class and cross-cultural movement among women. She learned to write — in the proper, Palmer method — at St. Mary's School in Dumont, New Jersey and Sacred Heart School in Bellevue, Washington.

Mary Moran, Métis – Ojibwe, was born in 1946 in the upper peninsula of Michigan. Her work has appeared in *IKON, Fireweed, Sinister Wisdom, Woman of Power, Ordinary Women/Extraordinary Lives,* and *A Gathering of Spirit: Writing and Art by North American Indian Women.*

Julien Murphy is 29, a philosopher and poet, who lives in Maine. She grew up lesbian, watching near at hand the toll of pregnancies and motherhood on the lives of her mother and sisters. Her first girlhood lover grieved often with her over the death of her mother on the birthing table for her younger sister. She came out at 23, finished her Ph.D. at a Catholic university, and has been teaching in Catholic and secular universities and writing about reproductive rights and lesbian politics for the past six years.

Patricia Novotny makes her home on the West Coast, thus maintaining a discreet distance from the Pope. She is a lawyer by training and a writer by yearning.

Pat O'Donnell, a native Texan, now resides in Tucson, Arizona doing spiritual direction/holistic counseling. At age five, she was an early convert to Catholicism and is still a practicing Catholic. She has a pastoral theology and Jungian psychology background, along with being highly intuitive.

Joy Christi Przestwor presently lives in the Bay Area. She combines her degrees in mathematics, women's theological studies, and business administration in her work as a Division Manager for a non-profit health care organization. She continues to celebrate her spirituality in an environment filled with challenges and opportunities for further human growth. Her priesthood expands day by day.

Maggie Redding gave up teaching to live a simple life with her partner and her partner's daughter in rural Wales, where they have no jobs and little money, but lots of fun, and reckon that's how life should be. She has written a novel, *The Life and Times of Daffodil Mulligan* (published by Brilliance, London), and contributed to *Walking on the Water,* edited by Jo Garcia and Sara Maitland (Virago). She is very cross with the Church and calls herself Catholic only to annoy.

Patt Saliba is thirty years old and was born in Texas where she still resides. She is a word processor and works with her family in the computer field. She lives with her companion, Eve, and three cats and a dog. Her interests include motorcycle racing, football and rugby, watching Bette Davis movies, and listening to the Blues.

Carol Seajay edits *The Feminist Bookstore News,** a magazine for feminist bookstore workers and women-in-print *impassionados.* Before that position became a full-time job, she worked in women's bookstores for nine years and started Old Wives Tales Bookstore in San Francisco in 1976. Her dream is to finish a publishable novel.
* Sample copies available for \$3 from FBN, PO Box 882554, San Francisco, CA 94188.

Joanne Still is a full-time freelance writer; prior to that, she held what her mother describes as "real jobs." She considers her Easter Duty to be the purchase of a Loft's chocolate bunny for the girl-children in her life, and her last good confession was the time she admitted to having an unexplained aversion to black-and-white bathroom tile (she has accepted the latter as a Mystery).

Fulana de Tal is the Spanish equivalent of Jane Doe. The name is used to identify the thousands of lesbians in Latin America who are presently forced to remain silent.

Crystal Waverly is a professor of human development at an East Coast university and a licensed psychologist in private practice who has worked extensively in the area of women's self-image within patriarchal religious traditions. At age 40, Dr. Waverly is currently giving birth to a book entitled *Silkworm,* a creative synthesis of reflections gathered along her psycho-spiritual journey. She is drawn to piano, plants, crystals, gourmet dining and cities. And passionately pursues the beautiful...and silence.

Jayne Young was born in 1958 in Hertfordshire, England, where she lived with her family until they moved to London when she was 13. She has lived, worked, and studied in London ever since, though she has fantasies of a quiet life by the sea ("don't we all"). She lives with her partner, Jackie, and two cats, Sappho and Spice. She is active in the Catholic Lesbian Sisterhood. She enjoys painting and drawing in her spare time — "when she has any."

Barbara Zanotti is a counselor, teacher and crafts-woman living on the north coast of Maine.

Selected Books of Related Interest

Allen, Paula Gunn. *The Sacred Hoop*. Boston: Beacon Press, 1985.

Baetz, Ruth, ed. *Lesbian Crossroads*. New York: William Morrow, 1980.

Beck, Evelyn Torton, ed. *Nice Jewish Girls*. New York: The Crossing Press, 1982.

Christ, Carol. *Diving Deep and Surfacing*. Boston: Beacon Press, 1980.

Cruikshank, Margaret, ed. *The Lesbian Path*. Monterey, CA: Angel Press, 1980. Revised and enlarged, 1985.

Curb, Rosemary and Manahan, Nancy, eds. *Lesbian Nuns: Breaking Silence*. Tallahassee, FL: Naiad Press, 1985.

Daly, Mary. *The Church and The Second Sex*. (With Feminist Postchristian Introduction and New Archaic Afterword). Boston: Beacon Press, 1985.

_____. *Beyond God the Father*. Boston: Beacon Press, 1973.

_____. *Gyn/Ecology: The Metaethics of Radical Feminism*. Boston: Beacon Press, 1978.

_____. *Pure Lust: Elemental Feminist Philosophy*. Boston: Beacon Press, 1984.

Fiorenza, Elisabeth Schüssler. *In Memory of Her,* New York: Crossroads, 1982.

Goldenberg, Naomi, ed. *Changing of the Gods*. Boston: Beacon Press, 1979.

Gramick, Jeannine. *Homosexuality and the Catholic Church*. Mt. Rainier, MD: New Ways Ministry, 1983.

Harrison, Beverly Wildung. *Making the Connections: Essays in Feminist Social Ethics*. Boston: Beacon Press, 1984.

Heyward, Carter. *The Redemption of God,* Washington, DC: University Press of America, 1982.

Kalven, Janet and Buckley, Mary, eds. *Women's Spirit Bonding*. New York: Pilgrim Press, 1984.

Moraga, Cherríe and Anzaldúa, Gloria, eds. *This Bridge Called My Back: Writings by Radical Women of Color*. Watertown, MA: Persephone Press, 1981.

Morton, Nelle. *The Journey Is Home*. Boston: Beacon Press, 1984.

Raymond, Janice. *A Passion for Friends*. Boston: Beacon Press, 1985.

Ruether, Rosemary. *Sexism and God-Talk*. Boston: Beacon Press, 1982.

_____. *Womanguides: Readings Toward a Feminist Theology*. Boston: Beacon Press, 1984.

Spretnak, Charlene. *The Politics of Women's Spirituality*. New York: Anchor Books, 1982.

Stanley, Julia Penelope and Wolfe, Susan J., eds. *The Coming Out Stories*. Watertown, MA: Persephone Press, 1980.

Starhawk. *The Spiral Dance*. San Francisco: Harper and Row, 1979.

———. *Dreaming the Dark*. Boston: Beacon Press, 1982.

Stone, Merlin. *Ancient Mirrors of Womanhood*. Boston: Beacon Press, 1982.

Swallow, Jean. *Out from Under: Sober Dykes and Friends*. San Francisco: Spinsters, Ink, 1983.

Organizations

Catholic Lesbian Sisterhood, BM Reconciliation, London WC IN.

Conference for Catholic Lesbians, P.O. Box 134, Highspire, PA. 17034. Networking and community building among Catholic lesbians. Publishes *Images,* a quarterly newsletter.

New Ways Ministry, 4012 29th St., Mt. Rainier, MD. 20712. Educational programs for the Catholic community focusing on lesbian and gay male experience. Publishes *Bondings.*

WATER (Women's Alliance for Theology, Ethics and Ritual), 8035 13th Street, Suites 1 &3, Silver Spring, MD. 20910. Retreats, workshops and resources for Christian feminists.